Brian Galvin
Chris Kane

Sentence Correction

Authors Brian Galvin
Chris Kane

Co-founders Markus Moberg
Chad Troutwine

Contributing Writers Neil Moakley
David Newland
Ashley Newman-Owens

Contributing Editor Jodi Brandon

Cover Design Nick Mason

Interior Design Tom Ahn
Dennis Anderson

Print Batch 2016.1

This book is dedicated to Veritas Prep's instructors, whose enthusiasm and experience have contributed mightily to our educational philosophy and our students' success.

It is also dedicated to the teachers who inspired Veritas Prep's instructors. The lesson that follows was only made possible by a lifelong love of learning and of undertaking educational challenges; we have teachers around the world to thank for that.

Finally and most importantly, this book is dedicated to our thousands of students, who have taught us more about teaching and learning than they will ever know. And to you, the reader, thank you for adding yourself to that group.

Personal Dedications

Veritas Prep is a community of educators, students, and support staff, and these books would not be possible without our cast of thousands. We thank you all, but would like to specifically acknowledge the following people for their inspiration:

Clay Christensen (Harvard Business School), Tom Cotner (Plymouth-Salem High School), David Cromwell (Yale School of Management), Lenore Goshorn (Allen Elementary School), Henry Grubb (Fort Osage High School), Dana Jinaru (Beat the GMAT), Patricia Kenney (University of Michigan), Steven Levitt (University of Chicago), Walter Lewin (Massachusetts Institute of Technology), Lawrence Rudner (Graduate Management Admission Council), Jeff Stanzler (University of Michigan), and Robert Weber (Kellogg School of Management).

VERITAS PREP

TABLE OF CONTENTS

CREATING *Think Like the Testmaker*

Creating is the top of the pyramid in Bloom's Taxonomy. When you have completely mastered the GMAT, you are able to Think Like the Testmaker. You are on top of the pyramid looking down! You don't just have good content knowledge and lots of practice with GMAT problems; you understand how a problem has been made, what makes it hard, and how to break it down. When you Think Like the Testmaker you can:

1. Quickly recognize what the problem is actually asking,
2. Discover hidden information and manipulate it to make it useful,
3. Recognize and see through trap answers, and
4. Create your own plan of attack for any problem.

APPLYING *Skills Meet Strategy*

What makes the GMAT difficult is not so much the underlying skills and concepts, but rather the way those skills and concepts are tested. On the GMAT, what you know is only as valuable as what you can do with that knowledge. The Veritas Prep curriculum emphasizes learning through challenging problems so that you can:

1. Learn how to combine skills and strategies to effectively solve any GMAT problem,
2. Most effectively utilize the classroom time you spend with a true GMAT expert, and
3. Stay focused and engaged, even after a long day in the office.

REMEMBERING *Skillbuilder*

In order to test higher-level thinking skills, testmakers must have some underlying content from which to create problems. On the GMAT, this content is primarily:

- Math curriculum through the early high school level, and
- Basic grammar skills through the elementary school level.

To succeed on the GMAT you must have a thorough mastery of this content, but many students already have a relatively strong command of this material. For each content area, we have identified all core skills that simply require refreshing and/or memorizing and have put them in our *Skillbuilder* section. By doing this:

1. Students who need to thoroughly review or relearn these core skills can do so at their own pace, and
2. Students who already have a solid command of the underlying content will not become disengaged because of a tedious review of material they've already mastered.

PREVIEW

As you learned in the Foundations of GMAT Logic lesson, the educational philosophy at Veritas Prep is based on the multi-tiered ***Bloom's Taxonomy of Educational Objectives***, which classifies different orders of thinking in terms of understanding and complexity.

To achieve a high score on the GMAT, it is essential that you understand the test from the top of the pyramid. On the pages that follow, you will learn specifically how to achieve that goal and how this lesson in particular relates to the ***Veritas Prep Pyramid.***

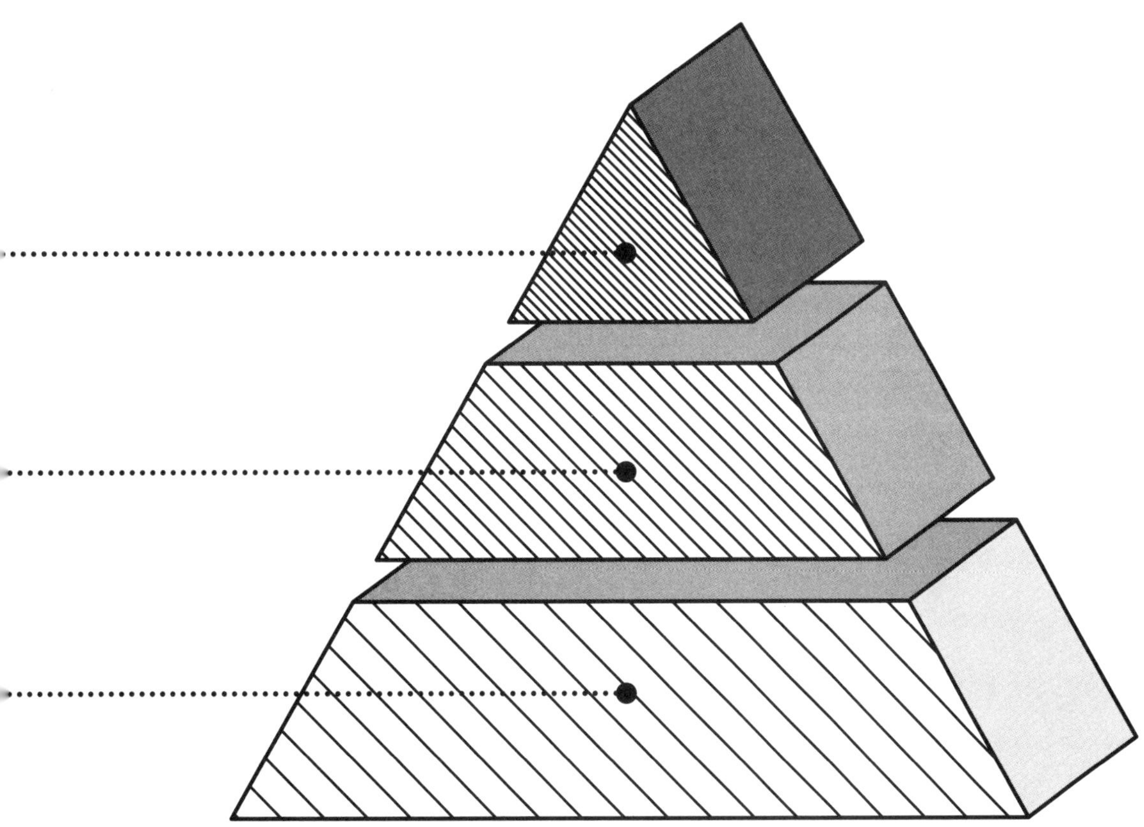

How This Book Is Structured

Our Curriculum Is Designed to Maximize the Value of Your Time

The Veritas Prep Teaching Philosophy: Learning by Doing

Business schools have long featured the Case Method of education, providing students with real-world problems to solve by applying the frameworks they have studied. The Veritas Prep *Learning by Doing* method is similar. In class, you will spend your time applying skills and concepts to challenging GMAT problems, at the same time reviewing and better understanding core skills while focusing your attention on application and strategy. The Case Method in business school maximizes student engagement and develops higher-order thinking skills, because students must apply and create, not just remember. Similarly, the *Learning by Doing* philosophy maximizes the value of your study time, forcing you to engage with difficult questions and develop top-of-the-pyramid reasoning ability.

An important note on *Learning by Doing*: In business school, your goal with a business case is not to simply master the details of a particular company's historical situation, but rather to develop broader understanding of how to apply frameworks to real situations. In this course, you should be certain to reflect on each question not simply through that narrow lens (Did you answer correctly? What key word made the difference?), but rather as an example of larger GMAT strategy (How could the exam bait you with a similar trap? How deeply do you need to understand the content to solve this genre of problem more efficiently?).

As you learned in the Foundations of GMAT Logic lesson, there are important recurring themes that you will see in most GMAT problems:

> **REMEMBER:** Don't mistake activity for achievement! Focus on recurring themes, not just underlying content.

THINK LIKE THE TESTMAKER

- Abstraction
- Reverse Engineering
- Large or Awkward Numbers
- Exploiting Common Mistakes
- Selling the Wrong Answer and Hiding the Correct Answer
- Misdirection
- Content-Specific Themes

SKILLS MEET STRATEGY

- Guiding Principles
- Problem-Solving Strategies
- Leveraging Assets

Each book in the Veritas Prep curriculum contains four distinct sections:

1. **Skillbuilder.** We strongly suggest that you ***complete each* Skillbuilder *lesson before class*** at your own pace, and return to the *Skillbuilder* when you recognize a content deficiency through practice tests and GMAT homework problem sets.

   The *Skillbuilder* section will:

   - Cover content that is ***vital to your success on the GMAT,*** but is best learned at your own pace outside the classroom.

   - Allow you to ***review and/or relearn*** the skills, facts, formulas, and content of the GMAT. Each student will have his own set of skills that are "rusty" or even brand-new, and will find other items that come back quickly.

   - ***Vary in length*** significantly for each book, based on the number of underlying concepts. (For instance, the Advanced Verbal lesson does not have a *Skillbuilder* because you are already building on the concepts introduced in three previous lessons.)

2. **Lesson**. The lessons are designed to provide students with maximum value added from an instructor by:

   - Doing in-class problems together (*Learning by Doing*), and

   - Analyzing those problems for the recurring takeaways.

     With each problem, there will be a detailed explanation that will help you understand how the problem is testing a particular concept or series of concepts, what makes the problem hard, and what underlying skills are required to solve it.

     When relevant, there will be particular boxes for *Think Like the Testmaker, Skills Meet Strategy,* and *Skillbuilder* when you should be focused on particular aspects of how the question is made or how the underlying content is being tested.

     NOTE: When doing in-class and homework problems, you should **do your work below the problem,** and you **should *not* circle the answer** on the actual question (just note it on the bottom of the page). That way, if you want to redo problems, you can simply cover up your work and proceed as if you had never done it.

3. **You Oughta Know.** The *You Oughta Know* sections will round out each lesson and cover:

   - Obscure topics that arise infrequently.
   - More advanced topics that are not common on the GMAT but do get tested.

   While these uncommon content areas do not warrant in-class time, we believe you should have some exposure to these topics before taking the GMAT. Therefore you should ***complete these sections before moving to the homework problems***. As with the *Skillbuilders*, the length of these will vary depending on their importance.

4. **Homework Problems.** In many ways, the homework problems are ***the most important part of each book.*** After refreshing core content in the *Skillbuilder* and then applying that knowledge in the lesson, you must reinforce your understanding with more problems.

   Each question is accompanied by a ***detailed explanation*** in your online student account, as well as a quick-reference answer key on the last page. A majority of questions are above the 50th percentile in difficulty, and they are arranged in approximate order of difficulty (easiest to most difficult). By completing all of the homework problems, you will learn all of the different iterations of how concepts and skills are tested on the GMAT.

   Homework problems are designed to be challenging, so do not despair if you are answering questions incorrectly as you practice! Your goal should be to learn from every mistake. Students can miss a significant percentage of questions in each book and still score extremely high on the GMAT, provided that they learn from each problem. Embrace the challenge of hard problems and the notion that every mistake you make in practice is one that you will know to avoid on the GMAT when every question counts.

SKILLBUILDER

The verbal section of the GMAT requires less underlying knowledge and fewer hard skills than the quantitative section does. However, Sentence Correction is the one question type on the verbal section that seems to require a vast amount of knowledge: the entire English language. As you will learn in the lesson to follow, the amount of knowledge required to do well on GMAT Sentence Correction is not nearly as vast as it seems. Still, you must be able to identify certain grammar and meaning errors quickly, and in preparation for the GMAT it is essential that you refresh core grammar rules. After years of using the English language, you should be inherently familiar with basic grammar rules and most grammatical structures. For native speakers, you first learned this information way back in "grammar" school, and for non-native speakers you may have learned much of this information more recently. Regardless of your background, this section will provide a series of mini-lessons and practical drills to refresh the grammar skills that are important for the GMAT and help prepare you for the full sentence correction lesson.

Grammar Terminology

Grammar terminology is intimidating and off-putting to most students, and understandably so. Do you know what a complement is? How about a relative clause or a participial phrase? Elliptical constructions, anyone? If you have a strong background in English grammar, you will be more familiar with these obscure terms, but the good news is that grammar terminology is not explicitly tested on the GMAT. However, to learn basic grammar and to understand solutions to Sentence Correction problems, you should be familiar with some important grammar terminology. What follows here is the basic terminology, and in each section relating to the different error types, you will learn some more difficult terminology associated those specific types.

WARNING! *This grammar terminology mini-lesson over the next three pages will not likely be fun for you. The intent is to provide a reference guide for you to employ to understand explanations over the rest of this book. Should you become drowsy or irritated, please flip quickly to the beginning of the "Different Error Types in GMAT Sentence Correction" section on page 22 for some Learning by Doing!*

Parts of Speech

In the English language, there are eight generally accepted forms of speech: noun, pronoun, verb, adverb, adjective, preposition, conjunction, and interjection. (As interjections are not important for GMAT Sentence Correction problems, they have been omitted.) Every word in a sentence can be assigned to one of these eight forms of speech. These forms of speech can be broadly broken into four useful categories: 1.) people and things; 2.) action or state of being; 3.) modifiers; and 4.) connectors.

1. People and Things

Nouns and pronouns refer to people and things and answer the question "who?" or "what?"

Noun: a word that is used to name a person, place, thing, quality, or action and can function as the subject, object, or complement of a verb, or as the object of a preposition

Example: *The **librarian** found the **book** and forwarded it.*

Pronoun: a word that takes the place of a noun (its antecedent or referent)

Example: *The librarian found the book and forwarded **it.***

2. Action or State of Being

Verb: a word that expresses action, existence, or occurrence

*Example: The librarian **found** the book and **forwarded** it.*

NOTE: There are two distinct types of verbs: action verbs and linking verbs.

1. Most verbs are action verbs that express some definable action. Examples are verbs such as throw, win, eat, write, etc.
2. Some very important verbs do not express an action but rather a state of being or feeling. Common examples of these linking verbs are is, seem, becomes, feel, etc.

3. Modifiers

A word or series of words (phrase or clause) used to modify something in a sentence. The exact part of speech of the modifier depends on its role in the sentence.

Adjective: a word that modifies a noun or pronoun. Adjectives are distinguished chiefly by their suffixes, such as -able, -ous, and -er; or by their position directly preceding a noun or noun phrase. Adjectives often answer the question "which?" or "what kind?"

Example: *The* ***brown*** *fox jumped quickly over the* ***lazy*** *dog.*

Adverb: a word that modifies a verb, an adjective, another adverb, or an entire clause. Adverbs are often identified by the suffix -ly. Adverbs often answer the question "how?" "when?" "where?" "why?" or "how much?"

Example: *The brown fox jumped* ***quickly*** *over the lazy dog.*

4. Connectors

Preposition: a word, such as **in** or **to**, or a group of words, such as **in regard to**, that is placed before a noun or pronoun and indicates a grammatical relation to another word in the sentence. Prepositional phrases typically function as adjectives or adverbs; the preposition establishes the relation of the prepositional phrase to the rest of the sentence.

Example: *Proper techniques and practice are both important* ***for*** *GMAT preparation.*

Conjunction: a word that links words, phrases, or clauses.

Example: *Proper techniques* ***and*** *practice are both important for GMAT preparation.*

To see all the parts of speech in a sentence, look at the following chart, which diagrams this sentence:

> *In the 19th century, doctors commonly used leeches as a remedy for all types of diseases and afflictions.*

prep.	adj.	adj.	noun	noun	adv.	verb	noun	prep.
In	the	19th	century,	doctors	commonly	used	leeches	as

adj.	noun	prep.	adj.	noun	prep.	noun	conj.	noun
a	remedy	for	all	types	of	diseases	and	afflictions.

Parts of a Sentence

In addition to the parts of speech, it is important to understand the basic terminology related to sentence construction. To form a sentence, the different parts of speech outlined above are put together in certain structures. Each of these sentence components will play a particular role in that sentence, and there is particular terminology related to them. The broadest and most basic components of a sentence are called the subject and the predicate. (In compound/complex sentences with multiple clauses there may be multiple subjects and predicates.)

Subject: The subject of the sentence is the thing or person that is perpetrating the action or executing the verb.

NOTE: The subject could contain multiple nouns or pronouns (compound subject).

Example: ***The big red house on the corner*** *is the oldest building in the village.*

The entire boldface section is the subject of this sentence. The simple subject (what will matter most on GMAT problems and what you will see commonly referred to as the "subject") is the one noun/pronoun (or nouns/pronouns, if it is a compound subject) without any modifiers that commands the conjugated verb. Here the simple subject is **house.** For subject/verb agreement, the simple subject is all that is important.

Example: ***John, my neighbor for 20 years,*** *is moving to New Jersey next month.*

The entire boldface section is the subject portion of this sentence, and **John** is the simple subject.

Predicate: This fairly confusing term relates to the verb and, depending on the school of grammar, most of what follows the verb. In simpler terms, the predicate is the part of the sentence that refers to the action relating to the subject or, if it is a linking verb, the state of the subject. In a simple sentence, it is usually everything other than the subject.

Example: *The big red house on the corner* ***is the oldest building in the village.***

The entire boldface section is the predicate, but the most important part of the predicate is the conjugated verb, known as the simple predicate. Here that is the verb **is.**

Example: *John, my neighbor for 20 years,* **is moving to New Jersey next month**.

The entire boldface section is the predicate, and the simple predicate is the verb **is moving.**

NOTE: For most GMAT Sentence Correction problems, it is only important to identify the simple subject and the simple predicate (the noun and the conjugated verb). However, the other parts of the complete subject and the complete predicate must be logically constructed and linked together. This will be discussed in the individual error types.

Other Important Terminology Relating to Sentences

Phrase: a collection of words without a subject and a verb

Example: *The big red house* ***on the corner*** *is the oldest building* ***in the village.***

Both **on the corner** and **in the village** are examples of prepositional phrases, perhaps the most common modifying phrases in the English language. Note that there is no subject and conjugated verb in these phrases.

Clause: a collection of words with a subject and a conjugated verb (a predicate). An independent clause is one that can stand alone as a sentence, and a dependent clause is one that cannot stand alone as a sentence and must be linked to other components to form a complete sentence.

Example: ***John lives in New York****, but* ***his wife lives in California****.*

The two boldface sections above are each independent clauses linked together with a comma and the conjunction **but.** Note that each has a subject and a conjugated verb, and each is a clause that could stand alone as a complete sentence.

Example: ***If it rains tomorrow****, I am not going to the park.*

The boldface section above is a dependent clause that contains a subject and a conjugated verb but cannot stand alone as a separate sentence.

Direct Object: a noun or pronoun (or a complete phrase or clause) that receives the action of the verb

Example: *I threw John* ***the ball****.*

What did I throw? The ball. The ball is receiving the action of the verb, so it is called the direct object.

Indirect Object: a noun or pronoun that indicates to whom or for whom the action of a verb is performed

Example: I threw ***John*** *the ball.*

To whom did I throw the ball? John. Since John is the person for whom the action is performed, he is called the indirect object.

Verbal: a word formed from a verb but functioning as a different part of speech. There are three distinct types of verbals, all of which are important to understand for GMAT sentence correction:

1. **Participles:** -ing or -ed verbals used as adjectives

   NOTE: Some participles are formed from verbs with unusual conjugation so they may not have -ed or -ing endings.

   Example: *The **crying** baby woke up his mother.*

   Crying is a participle modifying baby.

   Example: ***Bombarded by bullets**, the troops retreated.*

   Bombarded is a participle introducing a participial phrase **bombarded by bullets** that modifies troops.

2. **Gerunds:** -ing verbals used as nouns

   Example: ***Running** is my favorite activity.*

   Running is a gerund that serves as the subject of the sentence.

   Example: ***Driving to work** takes over two hours during rush hour.*

   Driving to work is a gerund phrase that serves as the subject of the sentence. The gerund **driving** is the simple subject of the sentence.

3. **Infinitive:** a verbal formed by placing "to" in front of the base form of a verb that is used as a noun, adjective, or adverb

   Example: *I like* ***to work.***

   The infinitive **to work** is a noun that serves as the direct object in the sentence. What do I like? **To work.**

   Example: ***To become an Olympic swimmer,*** *you must commit your life to the sport.*

   The infinitive **to become** introduces the infinitive phrase **to become an Olympic swimmer,** which serves as an adverb in the sentence—explaining why you must commit.

   Example: *The inherent desire* ***to survive*** *is an important trait in all animals.*

   The infinitive **to survive** is an adjective that is modifying desire and explains what type of desire is referenced in the sentence.

REMEMBER: Terminology is not important by itself, but it is an essential tool for understanding the grammar rules and errors that will be discussed in this lesson. Without an understanding of basic terminology and sentence structure, it is difficult to comprehend explanations for Sentence Correction problems.

Different Error Types in GMAT Sentence Correction

While there are many different errors in grammar, the GMAT tends to test certain ones over and over. In order to present the different error types, we have created an acronym—IMPACTS—that covers all the important errors you will see on the GMAT:

IMPACTS

- **I** — **Illogical Meaning**
- **M** — **Modifiers**
- **P** — **Pronouns**
- **A** — **Agreement**
- **C** — **Comparison**
- **T** — **Tense (Time lines)**
- **S** — **Sentence Construction**

For this Skillbuilder section, we will introduce the basic grammar concepts associated with each error type and use drills and examples to reinforce them. In the lesson portion of this book, you will learn how to apply this knowledge with strategies and real GMAT examples.

REMEMBER: On actual GMAT problems (as you will soon learn) you are not being tested on grammar in a vacuum. With the five answer choices, you are given important "Decision Points"—places where there are differences between the answer choices—that help to give away what is being tested and where the errors lie. In this section, the goal is to reintroduce basic grammar concepts (a little bit in a vacuum, but with drills and examples) so that you can more effectively assess Decision Points in the lesson portion.

Illogical Meaning

Often overlooked in Sentence Correction questions, illogical meaning is one of the most common errors in writing.

Incorrect: *Bill thought that the siren on his car radio was a policeman approaching behind him.*

People write and read this type of sentence frequently without noticing the incorrect meaning because they are not precise enough with language. Did Bill really think the siren was a policeman? No. What he thought was that the siren on his car radio was the siren on a police car approaching behind him. For a sentence to be correct, this meaning must be properly conveyed.

Correct: *Bill thought that the siren on his car radio was that of a police car approaching behind him.*

As you will learn later, the specific error that created the illogical meaning in this sentence is what we identify in IMPACTS as a comparison error. When two things are compared, it must be a logical, apples-to-apples comparison; in the original example a "siren-to-policeman" comparison is clearly illogical. Many specific errors that we will break down in this section are incorrect because they create illogical meaning. If you focus on meaning initially, you will naturally correct many of the different error types to be discussed shortly.

However, many errors of meaning are simply the misuse of language and do not relate to other specific error types. These can be broken down into three broad categories:

1. **Faulty Predication.** The subject and the predicate must be logically linked to each other or it is an error of faulty predication.

   Incorrect: *The main goal of the cellular research department at Johns Hopkins University is cancer.*

   This would mean, quite illogically, that the department's goal is to get cancer! To correct this sentence and make the predication logical can be done in two ways: changing the subject or changing the predicate.

   Correct: *The main focus of the cellular research department at Johns Hopkins University is cancer.*

   OR

   The main goal of the cellular research department at Johns Hopkins University is finding a cure for cancer.

   NOTE: Faulty predication is a common and often unnoticed error on GMAT Sentence Correction problems.

2. **Improper Diction/Improper Idiomatic Usage.** To properly convey certain meanings, it is necessary to use accepted constructions and be efficient in writing. When improper word choice or improper idioms are used, a diction (or idiomatic) error occurs.

   Incorrect: *I have the ability to play soccer.*

   "I have the ability" is awkward and incorrect, as there are simple verbs to replace that.

   Correct: *I can play soccer.*

   OR

   I am able to play soccer.

   Incorrect: *I will try and win the game.*

   You are not going to separately try and then win.

   Correct: *I will try to win the game.*

   Incorrect: *It's hard to choose between these appetizing desserts.*

   When dealing with more than two elements, among should be used.

   Correct: *It's hard to choose among these appetizing desserts.*

3. **Redundancy.** This is another type of meaning error that is surprisingly common in language. Redundancy can be thought of as a specific error of diction—that is, if the wrong words are chosen to express something, redundancy may occur. Here are some short, and often humorous, examples of redundancy:
   - close proximity
   - end result
   - plan ahead
   - advance warning
   - revert back
   - basic necessities
   - false pretense
   - personal opinion
   - join together
   - ATM machine
   - free gift
   - surrounded on all sides

   Incorrect: *The workers attempted to try to fix the broken circuits.*

   Attempt means "to try," so this is clearly redundant.

   Correct: *The workers attempted to fix the broken circuits.*

Illogical Meaning Drill

For the following 10 sentences, decide if the meaning is logical and clear. Four of the 10 are correct, and six of the 10 are incorrect. If the meaning is not correct, articulate the distinct meaning error(s) that exists in each one.

1. Doctors sometimes insist that their patients' illnesses are the result of depression, but in attributing these ailments to a psychological disorder, the patients are in effect told that these illnesses are all in their head.

2. Jonathan Swift wrote a newly discovered letter in the same year that he published *Gulliver's Travels.*

3. So persistent were John's inquiries at Harvard Business School that he was eventually admitted, even with a GMAT score well below the average at HBS.

4. Generally speaking, applicants give personal information in the essay section and list where they have worked on their resumes.

5. The news that many of us had expected finally came true.

6. The reason that the new GMAT books are so important is because the test is always changing and the curriculum always needs to be updated.

7. The argument over illegal immigration centers on whether illegal immigrants who have been living here for a long period should be granted citizenship.

8. The artist's rendition of the countryside is so unrealistic as to constitute what one critic calls an "alien landscape."

9. The car on the corner is identical with mine.

10. The directions on the medication recommend that you should take the pills with food and water at bedtime.

Illogical Meaning Drill Solutions

1. **Incorrect.** The second clause, which follows the coordinating conjunction "but," starts with the modifying phrase "in attributing these ailments to a psychological disorder." As you will learn more specifically in the modifier lesson (but you probably remember), this modifier must logically modify the subject that follows: "patients." Here is where the meaning error occurs: Is it the patients who are "attributing these ailments to a psychological disorder" or is it the doctors? Clearly this should be modifying "doctors," but it is easy to miss that in a more complicated sentence such as this. In complicated sentences, read each clause carefully and make sure that the meaning and modification are correct. Here is one way the sentence could be corrected by eliminating the modifier and replacing it with an "if" clause: Doctors sometimes insist that their patients' illnesses are the result of depression, but if these ailments are attributed to a psychological disorder, the patients are in effect told that these illnesses are all in their heads.

2. **Incorrect.** This sentence contains a pure meaning error that is easy to overlook. It is impossible for Jonathan Swift to have written a newly discovered letter—as if it was being newly discovered while he actually wrote it.

3. **Correct.** While this structure might seem unusual, it is a correct sentence and the meaning is properly conveyed.

4. **Incorrect.** If you read carefully, this sentence suggests that applicants list the locations where they have been working on their resumes—as in, they worked on their resumes at home, at the coffee shop, and at their friends' houses! Clearly the meaning here is incorrect and should read as follows: Generally speaking, applicants give personal information in the essay section and list previous employment on their resumes.

5. **Incorrect.** This is a great example of illogical predication. Can news really come true? No. It is a reporting of events or facts. A prediction could come true, but news "arrives." Here is that sentence corrected: The news that many of us had expected finally arrived.

   NOTE: Remember on the GMAT that you do not have to do this in a vacuum. In the different answer choices, the Decision Point of "has come true" vs. "has arrived" will be clear, and that will allow you to more easily consider the illogical predication in the original.

6. **Incorrect.** This is a good example of a redundant structure that is never correct. "Because" means "for the reason that" or "as a result of," so to say "the reason...is because" is redundant. This is a common redundancy error on GMAT Sentence Correction problems.

7. **Correct.** The correct idiom "centers on" is used to convey the proper meaning about what the argument is focused on. Also, "whether" is used properly to introduce a choice between two things. Remember: "Centers around" is always incorrect (how can something center around something else—illogical) and "if" is used for the conditional. Example: "If it rains tomorrow, I am not going to the park."

8. **Correct.** This fairly uncommon idiom "so x.....as to y" can be used almost interchangeably with the important and common idiom "so x....that y." This example is here for one reason: to remind you there are many idioms that you just don't know or that you think you know but don't. On the GMAT, difficult idioms are almost never tested in a vacuum; they are used to hide the correct answer. As you will learn soon with actual GMAT problems, never eliminate an answer choice based on an idiomatic choice first. Look for more logical and concrete Decision Points, and accept that the correct answer choice may contain a strange-sounding and seemingly incorrect idiom.

9. **Correct.** Same takeaway as #8. Almost everyone thinks "identical with" is incorrect, but it is actually preferred to "identical to" (which is also accepted by many editors). Again, realize how pointless it is to try to memorize idioms. There are literally thousands of idiomatic choices such as this, and the stated goal of GMAC (which oversees the GMAT) is to avoid testing obscure and difficult idioms. However, testmakers will certainly use idiomatic choices for misdirection, so it is *very* important that you assess idioms last when checking Decision Points.

10. **Incorrect.** Another great example of redundancy. The verb "recommend" means "to urge or suggest," and the word "should" has a *very* similar meaning. If you recommend, that essentially means that you should do something. This sentence should read: The directions on the medication recommend that you take the pills with food and water at bedtime. **NOTE:** This is a special type of verb discussed in the Tense section called a "subjunctive" verb; it requires a particular construction.

Modifiers

Modifier errors, along with comparison errors, are some of the hardest for students. It is essential for success on GMAT Sentence Correction problems that you learn modifier structures well, so spend some extra time on this section to make sure that you truly understand the different constructions. In a GMAT Sentence Correction problem, modifiers can play two roles: Either the modifiers are being tested explicitly, or they are being used as smokescreens to hide other types of errors relating to subject-verb agreement or sentence construction. To deal with the first type, you need to understand the proper use of modifiers, and to deal with the second type, you need to properly identify modifiers so that you can remove them from the sentence to assess other error types.

There are four important types of modifiers for the GMAT:

- Prepositional phrases
- Participial phrases
- Appositive phrases
- Relative clauses

Prepositional Phrases

As you learned in the "Grammar Terminology" section, prepositional phrases are modifiers that start with a preposition and contain an object (noun or pronoun). Unlike the three other common modifiers that we will cover, prepositional phrases can be adjectival (modify nouns) or adverbial (modify the action in the sentence). There are approximately 150 prepositions in the English language, so don't worry about knowing them all. Here are several of the most common prepositions: of, to, in, on, by, with, from, for, among, about. The good news with prepositional phrases is that people tend to understand them well, and tricky modifier questions hinge on prepositional phrase errors less frequently than on other modifier errors. Still, errors can occur when prepositional phrases are misplaced, and you must understand these scenarios. Before looking at some examples, you should understand two important things:

1. When prepositional phrases are serving as adjectives, they are almost always beside the noun, noun phrase, or pronoun that they are modifying.

   Correct: *The house* ***on the corner*** *belongs to John Smith.*

   Clearly ***on the corner*** is modifying the house.

   Incorrect: *The house belongs to John Smith* ***on the corner.***

   This would be incorrect as it is the house—not John Smith—that is on the corner.

NOTE: As you surely remember from grade school, dangling modifiers (modifiers that are too far from what they are modifying) are a very common grammar error. Most modifiers should be beside what they are modifying—*but* there are important exceptions.

2. When prepositional phrases are serving as adverbs, their locations can vary, and thus adverbial prepositional phrases are much more complicated. These modifiers have much more freedom of location, so they should be assessed carefully.

   Example: *Visitors to the zoo have often looked up into the leafy aviary and seen macaws resting on the branches, **with tails trailing** like brightly colored splatters of paint on a green canvas.*

   The prepositional phrase **with tails trailing** is telling us how the macaws are resting on the branches, and is thus adverbial in nature. It does not have to be beside macaws as it is modifying how they are resting.

Here are some examples of errors with misplaced prepositional phrases:

Incorrect: *Bill usually drops any groceries he has brought home from his job **on the kitchen table.***

All kinds of meaning problems are created by placing "on the kitchen table" in the wrong location. The goal of this adverbial modifier is to indicate where he drops the groceries. As it stands above, the sentence means that Bill usually drops his groceries (where? we don't know) that he brings home from a job that takes place on his kitchen table (as if he has an office set up on a kitchen table). Clearly, this prepositional phrase is poorly placed and creates a distinct modifier error.

Correct: *Upon coming home from work, Bill usually drops any groceries on the kitchen table.*

Let's look at another example:

Incorrect: *The Supreme Court recently ruled that the state had failed to provide some inmates at the maximum security prison with proper food and healthcare **in violation of the constitution.***

Again the placement of **in violation of the constitution** is problematic. The state—not healthcare—is the entity that is in violation of the constitution.

Correct: *The Supreme Court recently ruled that the state, **in violation of the constitution,** had failed to provide some inmates at the maximum security prison with proper food and healthcare.*

Participial Phrases

What is a participle? As you may recall from the terminology section, it is a verb form used as an adjective.

Examples:

- *The **crying** baby finally fell asleep.*
- ***Smiling,** the woman left the room.*
- *The **wrecked** car was sent to the salvage yard.*

What is a participial phrase? It is a longer modifying phrase starting with a participle.

Examples:

- ***Bombarded by bullets,** the troops retreated.*
- *Dogs **trained by professionals** are much more obedient.*
- *Kit Carson roamed the Rockies and the Southwest, **working as a trapper and establishing a reputation as one of the most able mountain men of his time.***

The rules for participial phrases are relatively straightforward:

1. If you start a sentence with a participial phrase, that participial phrase must logically modify the noun that follows the comma (unless there is another modifier inserted cleverly after the participial phrase). Example of a modifier error of this type:

   Incorrect: ***Alarmed by the recent decline of the stock market****, many retirement investments have been switched from stocks to more conservative options, such as money market funds.*

   Correct: ***Alarmed by the recent decline of the stock market****, many investors have switched their retirement investments from stocks to more conservative options, such as money market funds.*

2. If participial phrases are used in the middle of a sentence, they follow the noun they are modifying and are either set off by commas or not, depending on whether the information is essential to the meaning of the sentence.

   Examples:

   - *Dogs* ***trained by professionals*** *are generally very obedient. (essential to the meaning of the sentence so no commas)*
   - *The city's oldest church,* ***recently destroyed by fire****, has not yet been rebuilt. (extra, non-essential information, so commas must be used)*

   Incorrect: *Children, introduced to music early, develop strong intellectual skills.*

   Correct: *Children introduced to music early develop strong intellectual skills.*

3. When participial phrases are put at the end of a sentence with a comma, they are confusing because they can modify the subject of the sentence or the subject of the clause preceding it, even though they are not beside it.

Example: *Nadal beat Federer in five sets,* ***shocking the tennis world.***

Here **shocking the tennis world** is a participial phrase modifying Nadal. This sentence is a very common and important exception to the broad grammar rule that modifiers should be close to the noun they are modifying. This structure is used when you want to modify the subject of the sentence after you have learned something about that subject. By putting the participial phrase at the end, it necessarily links the two pieces of information. Nadal beat Federer, and with that action he was shocking the tennis world. Commonly, students want to change this sentence to: Nadal beat Federer in five sets and shocked the tennis world. This sentence, while not necessarily wrong, changes the meaning: If Nadal beat Federer and shocked the tennis world, then the sentence means that he shocked the tennis world with something other than the act of beating Federer. Perhaps he beat him and then shocked the tennis world in his press conference. If the goal is to show that Nadal beat Federer and that action shocked the tennis world, then the participial construction should be used.

Example: *Kit Carson roamed the Rockies and the Southwest,* ***working as a trapper and establishing a reputation as one of the most able mountain men of his time.***

This might appear to be an error of modification or parallelism to many students. However, the participial phrases at the end are properly modifying Kit Carson, even though the modifiers are very far away from the noun they are modifying. Because this is a confusing construction for many test-takers, it is used frequently on the GMAT.

While most adjectival modifiers should be beside the nouns they are modifying, participial phrases can be far from the nouns they are modifying when attached with a comma at the end of a sentence or clause.

Appositive Phrases

Despite the technical name, these phrases are fairly easy to understand and very common in the English language. An appositive phrase is simply a noun phrase that serves the role of an adjective.

Examples:

- *John,* **the lead singer of the band,** *has laryngitis.*
- **A gifted student and talented musician,** *John graduated from USC with highest honors.*
- *John spent last weekend visiting USC,* **his alma mater.**

As you might notice, these modifiers are almost always non-essential information, so they need to be set off by commas. Basically, the rules that govern appositive phrases are the same rules that you learned for participial phrases. The only difference is that appositive modifiers cannot be far away from the noun they are modifying. **Note:** Appositive phrases are often used to confuse students about subject-verb agreement or simply to make a sentence more complicated. If they are not part of what is being tested in the problem, simply remove them using "slash and burn" (a technique that you will learn later in the lesson) to simplify the sentence.

Relative Clauses

What is a relative clause? It is a subordinate clause that starts with a relative pronoun and is used to modify a noun. The most common relative pronouns that start a relative clause are: **who, which, that, where, whose, whom.**

Examples:

- *The boy* **who lives next door** *is my friend. (essential information, so comma is not used)*
- *Susan,* **who lives next door,** *is coming to the party. (non-essential information, so comma must be used)*
- *The dog* **that Bill found** *belongs to my neighbor. (essential information, so comma is not used)*
- *My car,* **which breaks down regularly,** *has become expensive to own. (non-essential information, so comma must be used)*

The most common mistakes relating to relative clauses take place when those clauses are used to modify action in a sentence or when they are placed too far from the noun they are modifying.

Incorrect: *It rained yesterday, which forced me to cancel the event.*

Correct: *It rained yesterday, and as a result I was forced to cancel the event.*

Incorrect: *The deposit that I put on the house, which is non-refundable, is in jeopardy if I cannot get financing.*

Correct: *The non-refundable deposit that I put on the house is in jeopardy if I cannot get financing.*

Important Strategy Tip: When you see a relative clause in any GMAT Sentence Correction problem, simply look at the noun before the relative pronoun and ask: Is this logically modified by the relative clause? If there is no noun or the relative clause does not properly modify the noun, then there is an error. While there are exceptions to this rule (relative clauses can sometimes modify nouns that are not directly beside them), you should not worry about them for GMAT Sentence Correction.

Modifier Drill

The following 10 sentences each contain highlighted modifiers. Six of the 10 modifiers are used incorrectly, and four are used correctly. Note which ones are correct and which ones are not, and try to articulate clearly the reason(s) why in either case.

1. John held parties for his kids **that featured clowns, numerous exotic animals, and lots of food.**

2. John held parties in his house **that featured clowns, numerous exotic animals, and lots of food.**

3. Bill Smith, the party's organizer, chose a variety of beautiful songs to end the night's series of events, **all written and performed by a local musician.**

4. In 1994, independent candidate Angus King won the gubernatorial election in Maine, **bringing to eight the number of successful independent bids for governor of a U.S. state.**

5. **Unlike water**, which is complimentary, all passengers need to pay cash for beverages such as wine and beer on the transoceanic flight.

6. Last year John performed well on the GMAT, **which gained him entry to both Harvard Business School and Stanford's Graduate School of Business.**

7. **Based on his experience in law school,** John recommended that his friend take the GMAT instead of the LSAT.

8. **On the basis of his high GMAT score,** John has decided to apply to Harvard.

9. **Best known for his role as Randle McMurphy in *One Flew Over the Cuckoo's Nest*,** Jack Nicholson's career has spanned over five decades.

10. **Politicians and philosophers,** the ancient Greeks pioneered early forms of democratic government.

Modifier Drill Solutions

1. **Correct.** Here the relative clause **that featured clowns, numerous exotic animals, and lots of food** is properly modifying "parties." Remember: "That" clauses are not nearly as strict as "which" clauses and can modify a noun that is not directly beside it. As you will see on the next example, you have to make sure there is no meaning ambiguity, but this sentence has no problems.

2. **Incorrect.** Here the relative clause **that featured clowns, numerous exotic animals, and lots of food** is illogically modifying "house." Compare this example to the previous one. There it was "parties for his kids that feature..." clearly modifying parties, because "that" cannot modify kids. Here it is "parties in his house that featured," so the relative clause "that featured..." is modifying "house." This clause is intended to modify the parties, so it is incorrect and should be written as follows: In his house, John held parties **that featured clowns, numerous exotic animals, and lots of food.**

3. **Incorrect.** The participial modifier **all written and performed by a local musician** cannot be put beside the noun "events," as it is not the events that are **all written and performed by a local musician,** but rather the songs.

4. **Correct.** Here is a good example of a participial phrase—**bringing to eight the number of successful independent bids for governor of a U.S. state**—that is attached to the end of the sentence in the same manner as the Nadal/Federer example. Angus King, by winning the election, was bringing to eight the number of successful gubernatorial bids in U.S. history.

5. **Incorrect.** The non-essential modifying clause—**which is complimentary**—is correctly modifying "water" and should be removed to examine the rest of the sentence. It is then clear that the prepositional phrase **Unlike water** is illogically modifying "passengers." The noun that follows must be something that could logically be linked to water, such as other beverages or snacks.

6. **Incorrect.** This is a classic misuse of a relative clause. It is not the GMAT **which gained him entry to both Harvard Business School and Stanford's Graduate School of Business.** It is the fact that he performed well that gained him entry. Remember: "Which" clauses must modify a noun beside it, and there is no noun in this sentence for the clause to logically modify.

7. **Incorrect. Based on his experience in law school** is a participial phrase starting a sentence. As you learned in the previous section, strict rules apply when starting a sentence with a participial phrase: It must logically modify the noun that follows. John cannot be based on anything, so this is incorrect. "Based on" is one of the more commonly misused constructions in the English language, so this sentence may not sound bad, but clearly violates a strict grammar rule.

8. **Correct.** This adverbial prepositional phrase—**on the basis of his high GMAT score**—helps the reader understand how or why he "has decided to apply" and is thus correct. In the previous example, "based on" is a participial construction and must modify the noun that follows. Because this is a prepositional phrase, it can modify the verb and can be positioned at the beginning of the sentence.

9. **Incorrect.** This is a classic example of illogical modification. Jack Nicholson is **best known for his role as Randle McMurphy in *One Flew Over the Cuckoo's Nest,*** but Jack Nicholson's career cannot logically be known for something. This type of error is very common on GMAT Sentence Correction problems, so always carefully assess modifiers starting a sentence.

10. **Correct.** This is an example of an appositive phrase—**politicians and philosophers**—starting a sentence. It logically modifies the noun that follows—"the ancient Greeks"—so the sentence is correct. This is a similar structure to: "A gifted student and talented musician, John made his family proud."

Pronouns

There are two distinct types of errors relating to pronouns: reference errors and agreement errors.

Reference Errors

Put simply, a pronoun should clearly refer to a specific noun (its antecedent).

Incorrect: *Green and Holmes played, and he scored a touchdown.*

In this sentence it is unclear if "he" is referring to Green or Holmes; the reference is unclear.

Correct: *Green and Holmes played, and Holmes scored a touchdown.*

Here is a trickier example of a reference error:

Incorrect: *Bill sent many e-mails to John while he was out of the office on vacation.*

Who was out of the office? John or Bill? Did Bill send the e-mails while he was on vacation, or did Bill send the e-mails while John was on vacation? This unclear reference creates ambiguous meaning and is a common error used on the GMAT.

If Bill was on vacation then the sentence should be:

Correct: *While Bill was out of the office on vacation, he sent many e-mails to John.*

If John was on vacation then the sentence should be:

Correct: *While John was out of the office on vacation, Bill sent him many e-mails.*

Reference errors can be subtle and tricky, but Decision Point analysis between answer choices usually allows fairly easy and quick recognition of this error type. Often reference errors on the GMAT are corrected by removing a pronoun and replacing it with a noun, or by completely restructuring a sentence as shown with the previous example.

Agreement Errors

In addition to having a clear referent, pronouns must also agree in number with their antecedents (either singular or plural).

Incorrect: *The average mother expects unconditional love from her child, and they are rarely disappointed.*

Here's the same sentence, corrected:

Correct: *The average mother expects unconditional love from her child, and she is rarely disappointed.*

Agreement errors can also be corrected by changing the antecedent and to match the pronoun:

Correct: *Mothers expect unconditional love from their children, and they are rarely disappointed.*

Pronoun Drill

Each of the following sentences contains a boldface pronoun. Decide if it is used correctly. If it is not, articulate the error. Four of the following 10 examples are correct, and six are incorrect.

1. On Tupac Shakur's single "Hit 'Em Up," **he** sampled the melody and tone used by the very artists he believed conspired to shoot him.
2. During the Cabbage Patch Kids craze, collectors were buying **them** for almost 100 times the retail price.
3. John played football with Holmes, and **he** scored a touchdown.
4. Mitt Romney did not mention the attacks on him for the tax return controversy during his recent campaign stop, but he did bring **it** up in an ABC interview last night.
5. The House of Representatives consists of 435 congressmen and congresswomen; **its** main purpose is to pass legislation that affects the entire country.
6. The campaign has to decide whether it should be more open about **his** past improprieties or simply avoid discussing them.
7. UCLA's football team was winning by 20 points, and **its** fans were celebrating in the stands.
8. By the time **they** won **their** 5th Grammy award, U2 was already considered the most popular band in the world by most critics.
9. Water rights on the Colorado River can be incredibly valuable; **it** is often worth more than the land itself.
10. Incredible homes line the Malibu coast, each more spectacular than **its** neighbor.

Pronoun Drill Solutions

1. **Incorrect.** In this tricky reference error, the pronoun "he" has no logical antecedent. Tupac Shakur is not a noun in the sentence, so there is nothing for the "he" to refer back to. This is tricky, because the name appears as a modifier—Tupac Shakur—but remember that a pronoun must have a noun to which it refers. **NOTE:** On an actual GMAT question you will have a correct choice such as this to compare to: On his single "Hit 'Em Up," Tupac Shakur sampled the melody and tone used by the very artists he believed conspired to shoot him. So it will not be nearly as hard to notice the reference error.

2. **Incorrect.** Similar to the previous example, this sentence contains a tricky reference error with the pronoun "them." "Them" is intended to refer back to the Cabbage Patch Kid dolls, but "Cabbage Patch Kids" is being used as an adjective and not as noun. It is modifying craze. What kind of craze? A Cabbage Patch Kids craze. From these first two examples the big takeaway is this: Make sure there is a clear and logical noun to which a pronoun is referring.

3. **Correct.** In this sentence there is a singular subject—John—and the pronoun "he" properly refers back to John. Many students will think that there is a reference error in this sentence because there are two nouns, but the pronoun must refer back to the subject, not the object. This sentence could also be simplified by eliminating the pronoun altogether: John played football with Holmes and scored a touchdown.

4. **Incorrect.** Ask yourself what the pronoun "it" refers back to. Clearly, it refers to the plural noun "attacks," so there is an agreement error. The second clause should read as follows: "but he did bring them up in an ABC interview last night."

5. **Correct.** The pronoun "its" properly refers back to the House of Representatives, a singular noun.

6. **Incorrect.** Here is another example of a reference error. The pronoun "his" has no logical referent in the sentence. To use "his," the candidate must appear as a noun in the sentence.

7. **Correct.** The pronoun "its" is properly referring back to the singular noun team. While "their" might sound more pleasing to your ear, it would be incorrect.

8. **Incorrect.** In the first part of the sentence, the pronouns "they" and "their" are used in reference to the band U2. However, U2 is then followed by a singular verb, showing that this noun is being used as a singular unit. While rock bands and teams are examples of collective nouns that can be used with either singular or plural meanings, those two meanings cannot be mixed and matched in one sentence.

9. **Incorrect.** After the semicolon, the singular pronoun "its" is improperly referring back to the plural noun "water rights". The clause should read: "they are often worth more than the land itself."

10. **Correct.** This tricky sentence is correct, as the pronoun "its" properly refers back to its singular antecedent each. It would be easy to think that the antecedent is homes and thus want a plural pronoun "their."

Agreement Between Subject and Verb

Put simply, plural subjects should have plural verbs, and singular subjects should have singular verbs. However, as with most things in grammar, it is not quite that simple. There are four distinct cases in which subject-verb agreement can be difficult to assess on the GMAT:

1. When the subject is very far away from the verb that it is commanding. The GMAT testmakers will try to obscure the proper agreement by separating the subject and the verb with a bunch of other structures, often very long modifying phrases that contain nouns that are not the subject.

   Incorrect: *The number of applicants to the top business schools are increasing every year.*

   The simple subject of this sentence is the noun "number," and the verb must agree with this noun, not any of the plural nouns that follow. **Remember:** Nouns that are objects of prepositions (in this sentence, "applicants" and "schools") can *never* be the simple subject of the sentence.

   Correct: *The number of applicants to the top business schools is increasing every year.*

   Here the simple subject "number" is properly agreeing with the verb "is."

   Here's another example of this type of agreement error:

   Incorrect: *Unseasonably warm temperatures in the U.S. and across Europe—particularly in the southern U.S. states and Scandinavia—has resulted in fears about drought and forest fires for the upcoming summer.*

   Here the simple subject of the sentence is "temperatures"—a plural noun—so the verb should be plural, not singular.

   Correct: *Unseasonably warm temperatures in the U.S. and across Europe—particularly in the southern U.S. states and Scandinavia—have resulted in fears about drought and forest fires for the upcoming summer.*

   NOTE: One of the core strategies that you will learn in the lesson portion is the concept of "slash and burn"—that is, crossing out all modifiers and extraneous words to isolate the simple subject and check subject-verb agreement.

2. When the subject is in the form "x or y," "either x or y," or "neither x nor y," subject-verb agreement is trickier.

   Incorrect: *Neither John nor his friends is going to the movies.*

   In sentences with the structures noted above—x or y, either x or y, neither x nor y—the verb should agree with whatever noun is closest to the verb. This is called "agreement by location" and is an important concept for trickier subject-verb agreement problems. Since "friends" is a plural noun and closest to the verb, then the proper verb should be "are," not "is."

   Correct: *Neither John nor his friends are going to the movies.*

   NOTE: When the subject is in the form "x and y," the subject is compound and will almost always take a plural verb. Example: Bob and his mother are going to the park. Here "Bob and his mother" is a plural compound subject that takes a plural verb "are."

3. When the verb comes before the subject. Normally, the subject comes before the verb, but often the subject and verb are inverted. Subject-verb inversion is a common structure that testmakers use to create confusing sentences in which it is difficult to pick out the proper subject.

   Incorrect: *Sitting at the far end of the bar is a local television reporter and one of the town's leading candidates for mayor.*

   What is the subject of this sentence? Is it "sitting"? "The bar"? Clearly, neither of these makes any sense, as the subject because neither "sitting" nor "bar" can logically be linked to the reporter. In this case "sitting at the far end of the bar" is not the subject but rather the complement of the sentence. The plural subject "reporter and candidate" comes after the verb "is" and cannot have a singular verb.

   Correct: *Sitting at the far end of the bar are a local television reporter and one of the town's leading candidates for mayor.*

   NOTE: When the subject comes after the verb, reread the sentence to yourself with the subject first in order to check proper subject-verb agreement. Here, read the sentence as: A local television reporter and one of the town's leading candidates for mayor are sitting at the far end of the bar. When you read the sentence with normal subject-verb order, it is fairly easy to check subject-verb agreement.

   Here's another example:

   Incorrect: *There has rarely been so many instances of mortgage fraud as during the housing boom of the last decade.*

   "There is/are" is probably the most common example of subject -verb inversion. In the sentence above the subject is not "there" but rather "many instances." Read this as "many instances has been there" and it is clear that the verb needs to be "have been."

   Correct: *There have rarely been so many instances of fraud as during the housing boom of the last decade.*

4. When confusing or unusual nouns/subjects are used. Often it is fairly easy to isolate the proper subject, but it is difficult to determine whether that subject is really singular or plural. Confusing subjects are not commonly used on GMAT problems but will appear from time to time.

   Incorrect: *A number of my friends is going to the movies.*

   Here the subject of this sentence is "a number" and the noun number is technically a singular noun. So why is this sentence wrong, and why does it sound so bad? Because whenever you use "a number"—a fairly common construction—it always takes a plural verb because the notional agreement (what we mean is many or several) takes precedent over the grammatical agreement.

   Correct: *A number of my friends are going to the movies.*

   Let's look at another example:

   Incorrect: *A thousand dollars are a lot of money.*

   Again, this sentence sounds terrible and is indeed wrong. But you should note that dollars is a plural noun, so why is the verb "are" incorrect? Because a thousand dollars is being used to represent one specific amount, so it "is a lot of money," not "are a lot of money."

   Correct: *A thousand dollars is a lot of money.*

   The broader grammar concept at play in these examples is often described as "grammatical vs. notional agreement." Usually the verb agrees grammatically with the subject, but in the cases above, what you mean—"many of my friends" and "one amount of money"—takes precedent in determining the proper verb. Because these cases must be judged on a case-by-case basis and can often be quite obscure, unusual subjects are not used often on the GMAT. Still, common examples such as the ones above might be used, and it is important to understand the broad concept.

Agreement Drill

For the following 10 drills, five have correct subject-verb agreement and five have incorrect agreement. Pick which ones are correct and incorrect and understand why. Remember that a sentence may contain multiple conjugated verbs.

1. One of every five people in the United States are obese.
2. Neither John nor his wife were very impressed by the film.
3. The failure of our country to enact financial regulatory legislation in the 1990s, along with numerous other missteps, was a major reason for the 2008 financial crisis.
4. Neither Edward's Market, which is located on Main Street, nor Prime Meats, which has several branches in the suburbs, carry grass-fed beef.
5. The combination of persistence, hard work, and luck is often necessary to gain acceptance at the top business schools.
6. Found among the ruins and wreckage were a gold necklace belonging to one of the victims and several other personal effects.
7. Patagonia, started by climber Yvon Chouinard in the 1970s, is one of those rare companies that has stayed true to the original vision of the founder.
8. *The Adventures of Huckleberry Finn,* one of the great American novels, is considered Mark Twain's masterpiece.
9. John, a career politician, along with his wife, one of the most famous political commentators, are starting a new show on CNN.
10. The growing tension between the two political candidates in the recent primary elections has been evident to all observers.

Agreement Drill Solutions

1. **Incorrect.** In this example, the subject of the sentence is "one," so the verb should be singular. One...is obese.

2. **Incorrect.** With the construction "neither...nor," the verb should agree with the noun that's closest to it. Here that noun is "his wife," a singular noun. The sentence should read: Neither John nor his wife was very impressed by the film. To most people, the verb "were" sounds better, but it is incorrect.

3. **Correct.** The simple subject "failure" is singular and appropriately matched with a singular verb "was." You should remove everything that follows "failure" until the verb "was" (you'll learn more about this Slash-and-Burn Technique within the in-class lesson) to check the proper subject-verb agreement.

4. **Incorrect.** This difficult example is testing the concept of agreement by location and has some garbage—the "which" modifying clauses—that need to be removed. With the construction "neither...nor," the verb should agree with the noun that's closest to it. Here that subject is the store Prime Meats, which is a singular thing. The verb "carry" is plural, so the sentence is incorrect and should read as follows: Neither Edwards Market nor Prime Meats carries....

5. **Correct.** The subject "the combination" is singular, so it should be paired with the singular verb "is." This is a straightforward example of focusing on the correct subject and removing unnecessary modifiers.

6. **Correct.** This tricky sentence is a great example of subject-verb inversion. The compound subject "a gold necklace...and several other personal effects" is plural, so it demands the plural verb "were." Because the subject comes after the verb, it is harder to identify and the plural verb sounds strange to your ear even though it is correct.

7. **Incorrect.** The main verb in this sentence is correct, but a problem lies in the relative clause "that has stayed true to the original vision." In a relative clause, when there is no noun following "that," the verb must agree with the noun to which "that" refers. Here that noun is "companies," which is a plural noun. As a result the clause should read: companies that have remained true to the original vision. **NOTE:** Subject-verb agreement in relative clauses can be tricky, so make sure you have picked the proper subject for the verb.

8. **Correct.** The singular book "*The Adventures of Huckleberry Finn*" is the subject, and the modifier that follows should be removed so that you read: The book is considered his masterpiece.

9. **Incorrect.** John is the subject of the sentence, and everything else is garbage. "A career politician" is an appositive phrase modifying John, "along with his wife" is a prepositional phrase modifying how he is starting the show, and "one of the most famous political commentators" is an appositive phrase modifying his wife. **REMEMBER:** After you have checked modifiers to make sure they are used correctly, you should remove them to check subject-verb agreement and sentence structure.

10. **Correct.** "The growing tension" is the subject of the sentence and requires a singular verb. Note the numerous plural nouns used in the modifiers before the verb, but don't be tricked by them!

Comparisons

Comparison errors are perhaps the most difficult errors to recognize on GMAT Sentence Correction problems. These errors can be subtle and are also common in writing, so they are easy to miss. For a comparison to be correct in a sentence, it must be logical and equivalent in form. Let's first look at a comparison that is incorrect because it makes an illogical, apples-to-orange comparison.

Incorrect: *Group A's findings are more significant than Group B.*

Put simply, a comparison error occurs when the sentence compares non-comparable things. Here it is clearly illogical to compare the findings of Group A with Group B itself. To correct this, the sentence must make a proper "findings to findings" comparison. There are two ways this sentence can be corrected:

Correct: *Group A's findings are more significant than those of Group B.*

OR

Group A's findings are more significant than Group B's.

While both are equally correct, expect to see the second correction on trickier problems, as it is not as familiar to most students. In the first correction, "those" refers back to findings and thereby produces a proper "findings to findings" comparison. In the second correction, "Group B's" does not need to be followed by the word "findings," as "findings" is understood, thus also making it a proper "findings to findings" comparison.

In addition to making sure you avoid illogical, noun-to-noun comparisons, you must also make sure to avoid action to noun comparisons.

Incorrect: *Software X crashes more often than Software J.*

In this sentence you are comparing the action of Software X crashing with Software J itself. Because the verb comes first, the comparison is clearly an action to action comparison and must be written as such.

Correct: *Software X crashes more often than does Software J.*

To many people, this corrected sentence sounds worse than the original, particularly the "than does Software J." In an action-to-action comparison, it is generally preferred to invert the verb (in this case, "does") and put it before the noun (in this case, "Software J"). This sentence would also be correct written as follows (but the inversion is preferred, and testmakers will typically use it to confuse test-takers):

Correct: *Software X crashes more often than Software J crashes.*

OR

Software X crashes more often than Software J does.

The other, and more difficult, component to proper comparisons is equivalency of form. When comparisons are made they should be logical—proper noun-to-noun, or action to action, comparisons of like things—and they should be in the same form grammatically. Consider this difficult example of a comparison error relating to equivalency of form:

Incorrect: *To imitate someone's success is not the same as duplicating it.*

Here the problem is not that the comparison is illogical, but rather that the forms are not equivalent. As you learned in terminology section, there are numerous forms of nouns:

1. Gerunds: -ing verb forms, such as running or swimming that are used as nouns
2. Infinitives: verb forms such as to run or to play that can be used as nouns
3. Traditional nouns: floor, car, wood, table, etc.

The infinitive form cannot be matched with other forms. Consider the following sentence, which does not contain a comparison error but rather a parallelism error:

Incorrect: *John likes soccer, basketball, and to play tennis.*

Here it is easy for readers to notice that "to play tennis" is problematic, as the sentence should say:

Correct: *John likes soccer, basketball, and tennis.*

OR

John likes to play soccer, basketball, and tennis.

In the original error example, the infinitive "to imitate" has been improperly compared to the gerund "duplicating," when the two nouns being compared should be in the same form. As comparing the infinitives would be awkward, this sentence should be changed to:

Correct: *Imitating someone's success is not the same as duplicating it.*

In addition to making sure that comparisons are logical and equivalent in form, also make sure you are using the proper comparison idioms.

Numerical Agreement

Singular vs. Plural (often described as Uncountable vs. Countable)

Singular	Plural
e.g., water	e.g., gallons
Much	Many
Less	Fewer
Little	Few
Amount	Number

Examples:

- There is less water in the Atlantic than in the Pacific.
- The Atlantic Ocean holds fewer gallons of water than does the Pacific.
- There is so much pollution in the air that children should stay indoors.
- There are so many toxins in the lake that it is closed to swimmers for the season.
- This lane is for customers with 10 items or less? WRONG!

Numerical Comparisons

Two vs. More Than Two

Two	More Than Two
-er (e.g., "better")	-est (e.g., "best")
Between	Among
The other	Another
Each other	One another

Examples:

- Kobe and Shaq are not fond of each other.
- The Oklahoma City Thunder are known to get along well with one another.
- I'm choosing between the chicken and the fish.
- That seat is taken; I suggest you choose another.
- It's strange: One shoe is in perfect condition but the other looks unduly worn.

Comparisons (vertical columns go together as expressions)

As	So	More/Less
Many/Much		
As	That	Than

Examples

- This candidate received twice as many votes as did any other.
- This candidate received more votes than did any other candidate.
- This candidate received so many votes that they didn't bother to count the absentee ballots.

NOTE: Comparison idioms make for easy wrong-answer creation. Simply "spin the wheel," and "as many as" becomes the incorrect "as many than." Learn to spot idiomatic errors that simply (and incorrectly) combine parts of these three expressions.

Comparison Drill

Of the following 10 sentences, decide which ones contain comparison errors and which ones are correct. Seven of the 10 are incorrect, and three are correct.

1. Like the Amazon rainforest and dense jungles that the black panther uses for hunting grounds and mating, the animal itself is disappearing as a result of clear cutting and expansion in these delicate ecosystems.
2. In-N-Out Burger is better than any fast food chain.
3. The average annual income of Malibu residents is about $250,000—about twice that of Orange County.
4. Unlike fellow Chicagoan Kanye West, whose recent records glamorize fashion, wealth, and excess, Lupe Fiasco's records stay central to West's original message, which provided social commentary through music and rhyme.
5. John has more money compared to Bill.
6. Burger King's recent advertising campaign, which involved a surreal and bizarre king presenting enormous breakfast sandwiches, was more successful than both McDonald's and Jack in the Box.
7. The new Burger King breakfast sandwich is as good or better than the old one.
8. Babe Ruth's batting records are more impressive than those of any other player's.
9. Except for Grover Cleveland, whose terms were separated by four years, all former two-term U.S. presidents served consecutive terms.
10. John's car breaks down more often than does Bill's.

Comparison Drill Solutions

1. **Correct.** Here the comparison might seem illogical at first glance. Can you really compare rainforests and jungles to an animal? Yes. With the words "the animal itself" it is clear that the goal of the comparison is to show that both the habitat (rainforests and jungles) and the panther are similar because they are both disappearing.

2. **Incorrect.** Here the error is subtle: Since In-N-Out Burger is a fast food chain, it is illogical to compare it with any fast food chain because it *is* a fast food chain. The word "other" is necessary to make it a logical comparison. The sentence should read: In–N-Out Burger is better than any other fast food chain.

3. **Incorrect.** This difficult example seems to avoid any comparison problems by having the word "that" in "about twice that of Orange County." But remember that in any comparison, you should ask the question: What is being compared? Here it is the income of Malibu residents with the income of Orange County—a nonsensical comparison. The second part should read: about twice that of Orange County residents.

4. **Incorrect.** After you sort through lots of modifiers and garbage, you can see that the core comparison is illogical: Kanye West is being compared to the records of Lupe Fiasco. It needs to be either a "person to person" comparison or a "records to records" comparison.

5. **Incorrect.** The goal of the comparison is to show that John has more money than Bill. Here an incorrect, and redundant, idiom is used: John has more...compared to Bill. Why is it incorrect and redundant? "More" already communicates a comparison between two things, so "more" is automatically "compared to." **REMEMBER:** In comparisons, using the proper idiom is important, and these idioms are listed in this section.

6. **Incorrect.** As in several previous examples, the comparison here is illogical. You cannot compare the advertising campaign of Burger King with the other chains. You must compare the advertising campaign of Burger King with the advertising campaigns of the other two fast food chains.

7. **Incorrect.** Like example #5, this sentence contains an incorrect idiomatic usage of the connectors in the comparison. By using "as good or better than," the sentence must mean "as good than or better than" —clearly incorrect. The correct idiom is "as good as," so this sentence would be correct as: The new Burger King breakfast sandwich is as good as or better than the old one.

8. **Incorrect.** This comparison suffers from a relatively common mistake. Clearly the goal of the comparison is to compare Babe Ruth's batting records with the batting records of all other players. It would be incorrect to say: Babe Ruth's batting records are more impressive than any other player. This would be an illogical, "records to player" comparison, so the second part could be corrected by saying: Babe Ruth's batting records are more impressive than those of any other player ***OR*** Babe Ruth's batting records are more impressive than any other player's. However, this sentence uses both, suggesting illogically that Babe Ruth's records are more impressive than the records of any other player's records.

9. **Correct.** This problem correctly compares Grover Cleveland to all other former two-term presidents. "Whose terms were separated by four years" is garbage that you should remove to properly assess the comparison.

10. **Correct**. Though it may sound poor to your well-honed grammar ear, this sentence correctly makes an action-to-action comparison. This car breaks down more often than that car does. Remember: In comparisons, it is preferred to invert the verb (put "does" before "Bill's") even if it sounds off-putting.

Tense

If you were to open a grammar book, the tense section might seem overwhelming. Past perfect progressive tense? Future perfect tense? The bottom line with GMAT Sentence Correction is that a basic understanding of the important tenses along with a focus on logical time lines will help you sort out any potential tense error. In this section, the basic tenses are reviewed, with a special emphasis on the past perfect, as it is by far the most commonly tested tense. After this section several more specific examples of tense errors will be given, along with a series of drills.

Summary of Verb Tense

Verb tense can be past, present, or future. In addition, each time frame has a perfect (or complete) form, a continuous (or progressive) form, and a perfect continuous form:

Time frame?	Perfect?	Continuous?	Example
Present	-	-	I study
Present	Perfect	-	I have studied
Present	-	Continuous	I am studying
Present	Perfect	Continuous	I have been studying
Past	-	-	I studied
Past	Perfect	-	I had studied
Past	-	Continuous	I was studying
Past	Perfect	Continuous	I had been studying
Future	-	-	I will study
Future	Perfect	-	I will have studied
Future	-	Continuous	I will be studying
Future	Perfect	Continuous	I will have been studying

The perfect tense is used to indicate an event that happened before an event in the simple tense. A frequently tested concept is the difference between the past simple tense and the past perfect tense. Map out the time line of events, and always use the past perfect for an event before another event in the past:

Jo discovered that Leslie had lied to her.

Leslie lied → Jo discovered → Now

As Mary shook Mr. Morgan's hand, she realized she had seen him before.

Mary saw him → Mary realized→ Now

Never use the past perfect ("I had studied") when you are talking simply about a single event in the past; always use the past simple ("I studied"). Also use the past simple with two events that happened at the same time in the past or with only one event in the past:

Jo discovered Leslie's lie.

As Mary shook hands with Mr. Morgan, she recognized him.

Jo discovered → Now

She recognized him → Now

Similarly, the future perfect ("I will have studied") describes a future event that will come before another event. The present perfect ("I have studied") simply describes an event that happened before the present. (A present event doesn't have to be specified.) The continuous tenses are used to indicate actions that are, were, or will be ongoing, often in comparison with another discrete event indicated by the simple form. For example: "I was studying in the library when the fire alarm sounded."

Perfect continuous tenses describe actions that occurred before another event and that are ongoing. For example: "By the end of the month, I will have been studying for 12 weeks."

Examples of Verb Tense Errors

Tense Error: In 2009, famed rock climber John Bachar, who revolutionized the sport with his daring free solos in Yosemite and Joshua Tree, fell to his death while soloing a relatively easy climb near his home in Mammoth Lakes.

In the sentence above, the time line is quite clear: In 2009 Bachar fell—an action in the past—and he revolutionized the sport before the fall. The past perfect is required, so that sentence corrected is:

In 2009, famed rock climber John Bachar, who had revolutionized the sport with his daring free solos in Yosemite and Joshua Tree, fell to his death while soloing a relatively easy climb near his home in Mammoth Lakes.

NOTE: If trigger words such as "before" or "after" are used—words that spell out the time line in a sentence—the past perfect can still be used but is not required. Each of the following would be correct:

Correct: *After Bill finished his beer, he went across the street for dinner.*

OR

After Bill had finished his beer, he went across the street for dinner.

Consider a different type of tense error:

Incorrect: *John was surprised to learn that most palm tree species were not native to California.*

This error of tense is more subtle and requires special attention to logic and meaning. The palm trees are "not native" at all times past and present, so using the past tense is nonsensical! If they were not native in the past, then that would suggest that they are no longer "not native"—clearly incorrect in meaning. Always use the present tense when you are referencing something that is always true or relates to a universal fact; these things are considered timeless.

Tense Drill

Out of the following 10 sentences, pick the ones that contain tense errors. Six of the 10 sentences are incorrect, and four are correct.

1. Before Clark left on his European vacation, he made sure that he had properly locked and secured his home and car.

2. After the accident this morning, the boy informed the hospital that his blood type was O positive.

3. When John told the school what had happened, the administrators had called the police and informed them of the situation.

4. In a school meeting, the principal demanded that students be quiet in class or face the consequences.

5. In the previous section, we are going to focus on several important error types.

6. After John returned from his trip, he realized that he had left his wallet on the motel desk.

7. It is essential that John does well on the GMAT.

8. Over 100 different pollutants have been found in the river.

9. 200 hours of community service must be completed by the defendant in order to pay back society for his crimes.

Tense Drill Solutions

1. **Correct.** When using words that clarify time frame, such as "before" or "after," you do not need to use the past perfect. This sentence begins with "before Clark left," so what follows will be a point before another point in the past. Because that time frame has been clarified with the word "before," the simple past "he made" is correct. However, the rest of the sentence is referencing a time before "he made," so the past perfect "had locked" must be used. On sentences such as this, map out the time line in your head and follow the proper tense.

2. **Incorrect.** If the boy informed the hospital that his blood type was O positive (using past tense), then that would suggest somehow that his blood type has now changed. When referencing something that is universal or always true, you should use the present tense and not the past tense. Corrected: After the accident this morning, the boy informed the hospital that his blood type is O positive.

3. **Incorrect.** Multiple uses of the past perfect tense are incorrect and create an illogical time line. The first part—"When John told the school what had happened"—correctly uses the simple past and the past perfect tense. The action that follows should be in the simple past tense (not the past perfect), as it occurred at the same time that John told the school. Corrected: When John told the school what had happened, the administrators called the police and informed them of the situation.

4. **Correct.** This sentence is not specifically about tense but rather about mood, an important component to verb form. The verb "demand" is a subjunctive verb that requires special verb conjugation. In the clause that follows, the base form of the verbs should be used—here, "be" and "face." This represents a different conjugation than if it were in the indicative mood, when you would write "students are quiet and face the consequences."

5. **Incorrect.** If the sentence is referring to something in the past—which it quite clearly is with use of the word "previous"—then the past tense must be used. In the previous section, we focused on several important error types.

6. **Correct.** Like #1, this sentence contains a word specifying time frame ("after"). Past perfect is not required in the portion following "after," and in fact would make the sentence confusing. However, following the verb "realized," "had left" is clearly referencing a point before that point in the past, so the past perfect tense is correct.

7. **Incorrect.** This is a difficult example of the subjunctive mood. Following an adjective expressing urgency, such as "essential," the subjunctive mood is required for any verb conjugation. As you learned before, the base form of the verb should be used, so the sentence should read: It is essential that John do well on the GMAT.

8. **Correct.** While this sentence is in the passive voice, it is perfectly correct. It is also a good example of when the passive voice is sometimes preferred—when the person or thing perpetrating the action is unimportant and/or the object is the emphasis of the sentence. Here the person or persons finding the pollutants is not important; it is just the fact that "the pollutants have been found" that is important in the sentence.

9. **Incorrect.** Here the passive voice is problematic, as it creates illogical meaning. By having the object as the subject, the sentence illogically suggests that the 200 hours of community service is going to pay back society for his crimes. While "passive voice" is not really a verb tense error, mood and voice are two other components of verb form that should be considered when deciding if verbs are used correctly. Corrected, the sentence would read: The defendant will need to complete 200 hours of community service in order to pay back society for his crimes.

Sentence Construction

Sentence construction errors form a broad category that refers to any error made by putting together components of a sentence improperly. There are three distinct subtypes:

1. Errors relating to punctuation when clauses are linked together or, more generally, how clauses are linked together

2. Errors relating to parallelism in a series

3. Errors relating to parallelism in common structures (not only/but also, either/or, etc.)

Punctuation and Linking Clauses

The most important punctuation mark to understand for GMAT sentence correction is the comma. Commas have *many* different uses in a sentence, but here are several important rules that are particularly useful on GMAT Sentence Correction problems:

Commas should be used when linking together independent clauses with a coordinating conjunction.

Incorrect: *Being unemployed can be difficult for anyone but John was having a particularly hard time with it.*

Without the comma, it is unclear where the new clause starts, and thus meaning ambiguity is created. It seems to say at first glance that being unemployed can be difficult for anyone but John—as if John is particularly tough and is the only one who can handle being unemployed!

Correct: *Being unemployed can be difficult for anyone, but John was having a particularly hard time with it.*

Commas should *not* be used when linking together two subordinate clauses, phrases, or words with a coordinating conjunction.

Incorrect: *John moved to the neighborhood only several weeks ago, but has already been invited to several parties.*

Correct: *John moved to the neighborhood only several weeks ago but has already been invited to several parties.*

In a comma splice error, a comma is used to join two independent clauses *without* a necessary conjunction.

Incorrect: *Bill has lived for 20 years in New York City, his mother moved there last year.*

Correct: *Bill has lived for 20 years in New York City, and his mother moved there last year.*

Correct Examples:

- The dinner was inexpensive and delicious.
- John lives in New Jersey but works in New York.
- John's neighbor moved from New Jersey but is originally from Maine.

NOTE: Pay attention to whether a proper coordinating conjunction has been used to link together clauses.

Consider this example of an error relating to choice of conjunction:

Incorrect: *The Amazon rainforest accounts for only 5% of the world's surface area and contains over half of the world's species.*

What follows the first portion of the sentence—"the rainforest accounts for only 5% of the world's surface area" —is clearly not expected, so "and" is an improper conjunction. The second part juxtaposes with the first, so either "yet" or "but" must be used, because what follows is so different or surprising in comparison to the first part. Remember: You will have Decision Points to help you note this type of error, as it is hard to pick up its own.

Correct: *The Amazon rainforest accounts for only 5% of the world's surface area yet contains over half of the world's species.*

Other important punctuation marks for GMAT Sentence Correction problems:

Semicolon: used to link together independent clauses (or sometimes for linking things in a series)

Example: *John wanted to keep the money he found in the briefcase; his conscience made him return it.*

Colon: used to introduce something that gives more information or clarifies what precedes the colon.

Example: *The Ponzi scheme concocted by Bernie Madoff was both enormous and complex: It took experts over two years to account for all the funds and understand where and how they were used.*

Dash: when a single dash is used to end a clause, its usage is nearly identical to that of a colon; when two dashes are used in the middle of the sentence, their use is nearly identical to that of parentheses.

Example: *The ESL class contains 15 international students—eight from South America, five from Africa, and two from Asia.*

Parallelism in a Series

Parallelism is a very important concept for GMAT Sentence Correction problems. Whenever series are presented in a sentence, strict rules of parallelism apply. Consider the following examples, which highlight several common errors involving parallelism:

Incorrect: *On his recent European vacation, Clark visited Spain, France, and spent an afternoon in Belgium.*

This particular error—referred to in some grammar books as "bastard enumeration"—occurs when two things are presented in a series and then the third does not follow the pattern but rather inserts a new predicate. If you write: Clark visited Spain, France, and…, what follows must be another country that he visited. If the goal is to express two different clauses it should be written as follows:

Correct: *On his recent European vacation, Clark visited Spain and France, and spent an afternoon in Belgium.*

Let's look at another example:

Incorrect: *The news report suggested that Mitt Romney would lose in South Carolina, win in Florida, and that he would dominate on Super Tuesday.*

This type of error—commonly called a "bungled series"—occurs when series are not linked together with the same grammatical structures or in the same form. All elements of a series should be in identical form. The sentence above should read:

Correct: *The news report suggested that Mitt Romney would lose in South Carolina, win in Florida, and dominate on Super Tuesday.*

After getting rid of any garbage, you can see that this sentence is really: The report suggested that Romney would lose, win, and dominate.

Here's another example of a bungled series:

Incorrect: *At summer camp, Johnny likes basketball, tennis, and to play soccer.*

Infinitives such as "to play" cannot be mixed and matched with other noun forms. This sentence could be corrected two ways:

Correct: *At summer camp, Johnny likes basketball, tennis, and soccer.*

OR

At summer camp, Johnny likes to play basketball, tennis, and soccer.

There are many different examples of parallelism errors, but the bottom line is this: When two answer choices on the GMAT present series in different ways, pick the one that keeps all elements parallel and in the same form.

Parallelism in Common Structures

There are particular constructions that demand exacting parallelism, and the GMAT tends to test these structures often. Some of these structures involve the following common expressions:

- Either/or
- Neither/nor
- Not only/but also
- Just as/so
- Range from/to

Whenever you encounter these common expressions, make sure that the structure that follows the first portion of the expression is identical with the structure that follows the second portion.

> *Incorrect:* *John will either win a million dollars on the game show tomorrow or he will walk away with nothing.*

In assessing the parallelism on this example, look at what follows the word "either"—"win a million dollars"—and make sure what follows "or" has the same structure. In this example" "win a million dollars" is not parallel with "he will walk away with nothing."

> *Correct:* *John will either win a million dollars on the game show tomorrow or walk away with nothing.*

Sentence Construction Drill

In the following 10 examples, seven contain sentence correction errors, and three contain no errors. Pick out the ones with errors and try to articulate the problem:

1. John recently moved from San Francisco to Los Angeles for a new job; a move that has made his children quite upset.
2. The recent rise in the stock market suggests that consumer confidence is improving and that the economy may finally be recovering from one of the worst recessions in the last century, but the persistent levels of high unemployment indicate that the situation may not be that rosy.
3. John works not only at the McDonald's on Smith Street, but also works at the Wendy's on Broad Street.
4. In New York City, vendors often sell merchandise illegally on the street, the subway, and in the parks.
5. The start-up is well funded, has two intelligent and forward-thinking founders, and a product that most experts think will revolutionize the industry.
6. The U.S. economy has been hurt by record unemployment and a prolonged financial crisis in Europe and therefore has struggled to recover as quickly as many experts predicted.
7. Most professional basketball players believe they are worth the exorbitant sums that they are paid and that the revenue they create for the teams and the league justifies the amount.
8. The company is running the promotion both to create new customers and reward its current ones.
9. On the GMAT, interpreting the question properly is often much harder than to solve the underlying math.
10. The root systems of most redwoods either become too crowded, resulting in reduced growth, or extend too far, causing structural weakness.

Sentence Construction Drill Solutions

1. **Incorrect.** When you use a semicolon to link clauses, the two clauses must be able to stand alone as independent sentences. The portion following the semicolon—"a move that has made his children quite upset"—is not an independent clause, so the sentence is incorrect.

2. **Correct.** In long sentences such as this, it is very helpful to "slash and burn" and read only the core elements of the sentence. In this example, you would read the sentence as follows: The recent rise suggests that this is true and that this is true, but persistent levels indicate that this is true. The sentence is properly constructed with parallel structures.

3. **Incorrect.** With structures such as "not only…but also," it is essential that you look for strict parallelism. In this example, the portion following "but also"—"works at the Wendy's on Broad Street"—must exactly match the portion following not only—"at the McDonald's on Smith Street." The verb "works" following "but also" is problematic, and the sentence should be written as follows: John works not only at the McDonald's on Smith Street, but also at the Wendy's on Broad Street.

4. **Incorrect.** Whenever a series appears in a sentence, make sure that each component of the series is presented in the same way. Here the second component—the subway—lacks the necessary preposition to make it identical with the other two components. The sentence should read: In New York City, vendors often sell merchandise illegally on the street, on the subway, and in the parks.

5. **Incorrect.** The error in this example is similar to the last one. A series is started; the company is_____, has _____, and _____. The last part of the series cannot just be a noun; it must be a third action (or, technically speaking, "predicate") to match the first two. This sentence should read: The start-up is well funded, has two intelligent and forward-thinking founders, and is selling a product that most experts think will revolutionize the industry.

6. **Correct.** As in #2, it is helpful to consider the core elements: The economy has been hurt by this and this, and therefore has struggled. The sentence is properly constructed, although the two elements are difficult to identify.

7. **Incorrect.** Again, "slash and burn" to see the construction error: The players believe this is true....but that this is true. The "that" before "the revenue" is incorrect. This sentence should be written as: Most professional basketball players believe that they are worth the exorbitant sums that they are paid and that the revenue they create for the league justifies the amount.

8. **Incorrect.** "Both...and" is another common structure in which strict parallelism must be applied. Here, what follows "both"—"to create new customers"—is not mimicked in what follows—"reward its current ones." This can be corrected in two ways: The company is running the promotion both to create new customers and to reward its current ones ***OR*** The company is running the promotion to both create new customers and reward its current ones.

9. **Incorrect.** Parallelism even applies when you are linking two things; these elements should be in the same form. Corrected: On the GMAT, interpreting the question properly is often much harder than solving the underlying math.

10. **Correct.** This is another good example in which you should slash and burn: The root systems either become...or extend.... This structure is perfect, but the added modifiers make it challenging for test-takers.

LESSON

Sentence Correction: Decision Points

If you give it some thought, you will find that the lessons you have covered to date are quite relevant to your role as a pre-MBA student. Arithmetic and algebra are fundamental math skills, and business decision-making requires quantitative analysis; the larger theme, problem solving, is a major facet of a manager's role. And logic and critical reading are clearly essential skills in the business and academic frameworks that you are about to enter.

But sentence correction? Grammar? As approximately one-third of the verbal section these questions will account for about one-sixth of your overall score. Why would grammar be held in such high regard by business schools?

You will see in this lesson why these problems are called "Sentence Correction," not "grammar": The GMAT is testing problem-solving and logical-reasoning skills under the guise of English grammar and diction. Logic and reasoning remain cornerstones of this question type and of this lesson. Effective communication skills are of course important in business and business school, so the GMAT does test some grammar knowledge, but it is limited to commonly known grammar principles, specifically those that relate to clarity of meaning.

While your grammar knowledge obviously matters for Sentence Correction, most people already have the necessary grammar skills to achieve a high score. What most people do *not* have, however, is the correct strategic approach to Sentence Correction, and that is the primary goal of this lesson: to introduce you to the concept of "Decision Points" and teach you how to effectively leverage hints from the answer choices to find the correct answer. By becoming good at core strategy and recognizing common errors through the use of Decision Points (and your "core competencies"), you will learn quickly that GMAT Sentence Correction is about effective problem solving, not chasing obscure and unimportant grammar rules (as so many people try to do in preparation for this question type!).

As you progress through this lesson, keep this axiom in mind: Sentence Correction is more about what you know to be wrong than what you know to be right. You are on a seek-and-destroy mission, eliminating incorrect answer choices and relying on the most common Decision Points to ensure that you eliminate safely and wisely. Your mission through these books is to become an expert at recognizing common errors and the structures within which the GMAT tends to employ them.

Sentence Correction and the Veritas Prep Pyramid

With Sentence Correction, there seems to be an overwhelming amount of underlying content: the entire English language. But it is important to remember that the GMAT tests a relatively narrow scope of grammatical errors, and that set relies largely on logical meaning. Still, you must have a mastery of the grammatical concepts that the GMAT does test, **so the Skillbuilder is particularly important for this lesson. Use the targeted grammar review sections and drills to make sure you have the requisite grammar knowledge**.

In class, you will focus mainly on "Learning by Doing"; you will see how to attack problems strategically while learning important GMAT grammar rules through the problems themselves. Only then you will start to understand how the testmakers make Sentence Correction hard and how to approach this exercise properly. Perhaps more than any other problem type, Sentence Correction is an even mix of the three pyramid levels. You need core grammar knowledge (bottom), strategies for attacking the problems (middle), and a deep understanding of how testmakers bait you into certain mistakes (top). **Overall, however, students preparing for Sentence Correction spend way too much time on the bottom of the pyramid at the expense of good strategy.** Broadening your base of grammar knowledge beyond the core skills outlined in the Skillbuilder is a poor use of time and is unlikely to change your score significantly. **However, if you improve your strategy and learn how to "Think Like the Testmaker," you will see enormous gains in your Sentence Correction abilities.** The following are the core concepts/skills for Sentence Correction from the Veritas Prep Pyramid:

"Core Skills" from Skillbuilder:

- Grammar Rules by Error Type (IMPACTS)
- Basic Strategy

"Skills Meet Strategy" Takeaways from the Lesson Section

- Decision Points
- Slash and Burn
- Use it or Lose It
- Learning by Doing

"Think Like the Testmaker" Takeaways from the Lesson Section

- Selling the Wrong Answer
- Hiding the Correct Answer
- Misdirection
- Abstraction
- Content-Specific Themes

Sentence Correction Deconstructed

Before examining the core strategies for success on Sentence Correction, let's review the question type and official instructions for Sentence Correction on the GMAT:

Official Directions: The question presents a sentence, part of which or all of which is underlined.

Beneath the sentence you will find five ways of phrasing the underlined part. The first of these repeats the original; the other four are different. If you think the original is best, choose the first answer; otherwise choose one of the others.

This question tests correctness and effectiveness of expression. In choosing your answer, follow the requirements of standard written English; that is, pay attention to grammar, choice of words, and sentence construction. **Choose the answer that produces the most effective sentence; this answer should be clear and exact, without awkwardness, ambiguity, redundancy, or grammatical error.**

Anatomy of a Sentence Correction Problem

While market-driven competition encourages pharmaceutical companies to actively seek innovative new drugs, market analysts note that marketing accounts for twice as much of the industry budget as research.

(A) marketing accounts for twice as much of the industry budget as research

(B) marketing accounts for twice as much of the industry budget as does research

(C) the industry budget is accounted for twice as much by marketing than research

(D) the industry budget is accounted for twice as much by marketing than by research

(E) marketing new drugs is twice as expensive compared to research

SECTION 1: SENTENCE CORRECTION STRATEGY

Decision Points: Answer Choices as Assets

At this point in the course, you have probably realized that the GMAT is designed mainly to assess who is good at leveraging information to make the best decisions (which is the heart of problem solving!). To leverage information well on the GMAT, you must have good content understanding, but you also need to be effective at recognizing hints within the question stem and the answer choices. In no other question type is this more important than in Sentence Correction.

The "Decision Points" strategy highlighted on the next few pages is built exclusively on the idea that the answer choices are assets. **In every difference that the testmakers provide between the individual answer choices, they are giving you important hints about what might be wrong.** To highlight how important these differences are in the game of sentence correction, consider two sentences without choices to see if you can figure out if they are correct or incorrect:

1. **Although the term "psychopath" is popularly applied to an especially brutal criminal, in psychology it is someone who is apparently incapable of feeling compassion or the pangs of conscience.**

2. **Five fledgling sea eagles left their nests in western Scotland this summer, bringing to 34 the number of wild birds successfully raised since transplants from Norway began in 1975.**

These are tough decisions, aren't they? Sentence correction is extremely difficult in a vacuum, especially when you need to scan the entire sentence for any possible error. In this case, the bar for "correct" is set at "100% correct," with any one tiny error making the sentence "incorrect." This process is tedious and even nerve-wracking. Admit it: You began to doubt even simple structures that you commonly use. **The problem? Without choices there is no context for you to gain a foothold or see a starting point. But remember this: The GMAT does not give you "true/false" Sentence Correction problems.**

This is why, on the GMAT, you should embrace the multiple-choice construct. These long sentences are difficult to assess on their own, **but the GMAT format gives you five answer choices against which you can play the differences. This is what makes Sentence Correction a problem-solving exercise.** "Grammar" is a field in which very few pre-MBAs would consider themselves experts, but decision-making is something you can do proficiently with practice. Therefore, you should play the answer choices against each other, looking for "Decision Points." Try these same two examples on the next page with some context:

Now let's revisit those two sentences in a true Sentence Correction context. Decide which one is correct:

1. Although the term "psychopath" is popularly applied to an especially brutal criminal, in psychology it is someone who is apparently incapable of feeling compassion or the pangs of conscience.

   vs.

   Although the term "psychopath" is popularly applied to an especially brutal criminal, in psychology it refers to someone who is apparently incapable of feeling compassion or the pangs of conscience.

2. Five fledgling sea eagles left their nests in western Scotland this summer, bringing to 34 the number of wild birds successfully raised since transplants from Norway began in 1975.

   vs.

   Five fledgling sea eagles left their nests in western Scotland this summer, and it brought to 34 the number of wild birds successfully raised since transplants from Norway began in 1975.

LEARNING BY DOING

Leverage the Choices and Focus on Core Competencies

Most likely, this second exercise felt much more comfortable for you. You know what decisions you are being asked to make and hints are given. In example #1 above, the obvious choice between "it is" versus "it refers" reminds you that "a term" cannot be someone, but it can refer to someone. Therefore the original on the previous page was incorrect, and the changed version on this page is correct. But did you notice that on your own? Probably not! The second example contains a structure "bringing to 34…" that most students think is incorrect. But if you had to choose between the sentences in #2 above, which one would you pick? The second is clearly wrong! The pronoun "it" has no logical antecedent in the sentence, so you are left to pick the one you probably thought was wrong on the previous page. The decisions above are relatively straightforward if you take the hints that you are given and eliminate what you know to be wrong; on the previous page, those decisions were anything but straightforward.

SKILLS MEET STRATEGY

Focus on Core Competencies

If you'll go with the analogy, GMAT questions are a lot like the business cases that you will use in your MBA program. They are situations that may seem a bit abstract in isolation (unless you have a time machine, you'll never become CEO of Xerox in 1982), but from which larger lessons can be learned (that situation that Xerox faced can teach you about business principles that will help you down the road). Sentence Correction questions are terrific microcosms of the business concept of core competencies, in that they are written to coax you toward making decisions (or taking on initiatives) that most are simply unqualified to make reliably. By mastering and looking for common GMAT Decision Points, you can avoid the temptation to chase the "perfect sentence," and you can efficiently and effectively solve problems, much as an effective manager would.

The Decision Point Process

Now that you understand the game of leveraging answer choices, let's summarize the core process for attacking any Sentence Correction problem:

1. **Briefly scan for obvious differences** between answer choices.

   You'll learn to note the most common Decision Points:

   - The first and last words of the answer choices
   - "**Low-hanging fruit"** such as pronouns ("it" vs. "they" is a classic decision point) and verbs (have vs. has; was vs. had been; verb differences can mean either subject-verb agreement or verb tense errors, but noting two forms of the same verb should clue you in to a decision point regardless)

2. **Read the sentence carefully**, mining it for any common grammar errors (represented by IMPACTS on the next page).

   When you find a clear error, go through the answer choices to eliminate each occurrence of that error.

3. **Eliminate incorrect answer choices, but *only* when you are absolutely certain that you have found an error.**

   Beware of false "Decision Points." By far the most common error that students make when using process of elimination is eliminating answers that "don't sound right" or that don't fit their idea of the preferred way to communicate that sentence. One of the GMAT's great weapons against you is correct-but-unusual sentence structure or choice of diction.

   Whenever you can quickly recognize obvious differences, you might as well read specifically for those, but do not fret if a Decision Point does not immediately present itself. You will arrive at Decision Points as you read through the answer choices.

   On the next page and the pages that follow, you will learn the different error types and how to recognize them quickly in the Sentence Correction context.

IMPACTS Error Types

To properly assess Decision Points, you must understand important grammar rules. To do that, it is helpful to categorize those rules in some logical way. The GMAT tests the following families of errors, organized by the acronym "IMPACTS":

Illogical Meaning

Modifiers

Pronouns

Agreement (Between Subject-Verb)

Comparisons

Tenses (or Time Lines)

Sentence Construction

Over time, you will become familiar with these error families and understand how testmakers like to test them by doing several examples of each. If you find that you do not understand the grammar associated with any of these categories, make sure that you revisit the Skillbuilder, where they are presented with detailed examples.

Sentence Correction Strategy Summary

Without question, Sentence Correction is the most misunderstood problem type on the GMAT. Remember: It is not so much a test of grammar as it is a problem-solving exercise based in language. **Learning obscure grammar in a vacuum will not help you on Sentence Correction problems, but mastering good strategy will give you a huge competitive advantage over other test-takers.** To succeed on Sentence Correction problems, focus on the following points:

- Sentence correction is mainly about leveraging hints from the answer choices. Make sure you assess every single difference that exists between the answer choices. **People tend to get questions wrong not because they don't understand the grammar, but because they didn't leverage every single difference between answer choices.**

- **The game of Sentence Correction is process of elimination.** Focus on what you know to be wrong, not what you think is correct. Make sure that you focus on the "low-hanging fruit" first and eliminate the most obvious incorrect options before moving to difficult decision points.

- **Only eliminate answer choices when you are sure they are incorrect.** This is absolutely essential to the Decision Points strategy. Testmakers will bait you into eliminating answer choices that contain unusual structures or unique scenarios with which you are not familiar but that are actually correct; don't fall for it! **If you are not sure of one Decision Point, keep looking for others.**

- **Sentence Correction problems test the same core grammar rules over and over again.** They are rarely difficult because of the rules themselves, but because of the way those rules are presented. Focus on the core grammar rules and how they are tested, not obscure grammar.

- **Sentence Correction is about Learning by Doing.** If you get a problem wrong, you should determine if you missed it because you do not understand a grammar rule or because you used bad strategy. Most people miss problems more because of bad strategy than an underlying weakness in content. However, if you do not understand some important grammar content and miss a problem because of that, you should take the time to learn that content thoroughly.

- **Only focus on Decision Points that matter**. People spend way too much time considering differences that do not need to be assessed or that do not matter in determining the correct answer. Remember: There are many "false" Decision Points (ones that do not matter, ones you do not know, or ones in which both options are correct or incorrect), so focus primarily on core competencies and the easier Decision Points first.
- Know that difficult decisions are often more about meaning than about rules, and that that is a good thing for you. **When you are faced with a difficult choice, consider the meaning behind each option and you will often find that the decision is clearer.** After all, the purpose of grammar is to ensure that language conveys clear meaning. What may be a technically correct sentence grammatically may often have an illogical meaning, so it is essential to keep that in mind.

SECTION 2: IMPACTS ERRORS: LEARNING BY DOING

For the remainder of the lesson, you will review the core IMPACTS error types through the lens of difficult problems. Each section will start with a review from the Skillbuilder that highlights common errors for that one family. For the problems that follow, you should focus on both important strategy takeaways and underlying grammar. Certain error types require certain strategies, and those will be particularly emphasized when appropriate. Also know that almost every GMAT Sentence Correction problem tests multiple families of errors, so you will see more than just the type you are covering in that section.

Illogical Meaning

The first error, illogical meaning, is a capstone for the entire genre of sentence correction; **as you will see, most IMPACTS errors will create illogical or unclear meanings.** With every Decision Point you assess, you should ask yourself whether a meaning error is present. Before you see this error in several full questions, let's review the core grammar skills relating to Illogical meaning.

ILLOGICAL MEANING: CORE CONCEPTS FROM SKILLBUILDER

1. Faulty predication—the subject and predicate must be logically linked to each other or it is an error of faulty predication.

   Incorrect: ***The main goal of the cellular research department at Johns Hopkins University is cancer.***

   Correct: ***The main goal of the cellular research department at Johns Hopkins University is finding a cure for cancer.***

2. Improper diction—to properly convey certain meanings, it is necessary to use accepted constructions and be efficient in writing. When improper word choice or improper idioms are used, a diction (or idiomatic) error occurs.

   Incorrect: ***I will try and win the game.***

   Correct: ***I will try to win the game.***

3. Redundancy—another type of meaning error that is surprisingly common. Redundancy can be thought of as a specific error of diction—that is, if the wrong words are chosen to express something, redundancy may occur.

   Incorrect: ***The art portfolio depreciated in value by 20%.***

   Correct: ***The art portfolio depreciated by 20%.***

1. The dolphin, one of nature's most intelligent animals, has been known to cover its snout with ocean sponges to better forage for food, <u>in effect creating their own farming equipment</u>.

(A) in effect creating their own farming equipment

(B) so that it creates its own farming equipment

(C) so that they create their own farming equipment

(D) in effect creating its own farming equipment

(E) creating effective farming equipment

LEARNING BY DOING
Meaning Errors Can Be Subtle

The first Decision Point that you should analyze on this problem is a relatively easy one: the choice between the pronouns "its" and "their." Since "the dolphin" is singular, the plural "their" is wrong, and you can safely eliminate answer choices A and C. The choices between the remaining three are a bit more nuanced and difficult to leverage. They deal specifically with illogical meaning and the question of whether dolphins really "create equipment." Of course not! Farming is an agricultural process that takes place on land, and farming equipment refers to a known set of tools and machines created and employed by humans. To be logical, the sentence must be metaphorical rather than literal; thus, an answer choice that reads "...so that it creates its own farming equipment" is illogical, and one that says "creating effective farm equipment" is even worse; not only are they illogically creating farming equipment but it's very effective farming equipment! Only answer choice D makes the expression a metaphor and is thus correct.

Illogical meaning can be subtle, but remember that you don't need to detect meaning errors in a vacuum; you will always have answer choices that you can compare, keeping meaning in mind. The Decision Points question that you should ask on this problem is: Why did they give a choice of "in effect" vs. "so that"?

SKILLS MEET STRATEGY
Logical Meaning Is Your Primary Goal

Going forward, remember that logical meaning is your primary goal in assessing sentences and that many grammatical errors relate to meaning. Often GMAT students become so enamored of grammatical rules (particularly those related to agreement) that they select choices that "look" grammatically correct but that supply blatantly illogical meanings. Make sure that logical meaning is a primary emphasis as you assess each answer choice.

SKILLBUILDER

- Pronoun—agreement
- Illogical meaning—diction

2. <u>In contrast to 19th-century wars, in which most casualties resulted from disease, over two-thirds of the troops killed on the battlefield in World War I resulted from direct combat.</u>

(A) In contrast to 19th-century wars, in which most casualties resulted from disease, over two-thirds of the troops killed on the battlefield in World War I resulted from direct combat.

(B) In contrast to 19th-century wars, in which most casualties resulted from disease, World War I had over two-thirds of its troops killed from direct combat on the battlefield.

(C) In contrast to troops in 19th-century wars, in which most casualties resulted from disease, over two-thirds of the troops killed on the battlefield in World War I resulted from direct combat.

(D) While most casualties in 19th-century wars resulted from disease, over two-thirds of the troops killed on the battlefield in World War I resulted from direct combat.

(E) Whereas most casualties in 19th-century wars resulted from disease, over two-thirds of the casualties in World War I resulted from direct combat on the battlefield.

LEARNING BY DOING
Faulty Predication

On this problem, the easiest Decision Point is a meaning error that relates to the comparison family of errors. In the original sentence, there is an illogical comparison: "In contrast to 19th-century wars...troops" is wrong, because you can't compare wars to troops. So answer choice A can be eliminated. Answer choice B corrects that comparison problem ("In contrast to 19th-century wars...World War I" is a logical war-to-war comparison) but illogically uses "its troops" as if WWI possessed the troops. Again this is illogical in meaning, so answer choice B can be eliminated. Answer choices C and D both contain subtler errors of faulty predication; you cannot say "two-thirds of the troops killed resulted from direct combat." The troops did not result from combat; the casualties did. Answer choice E corrects that problem and is the only one with logical meaning.

SKILLS MEET STRATEGY
It Takes Time to Assess Decision Points Properly

Heed these important words: If you rush the Decision Point process, you will miss many questions that you should have gotten right. It takes time to find the Decision Points in this example, as there are many changes between the answer choices. Make sure that you always take the time to find all Decision Points in a question and properly leverage the hints you are given.

THINK LIKE THE TESTMAKER
Misdirection and Hiding the Correct Answer

As you do the problems in this lesson, it is essential that you focus on what makes each of them hard, particularly those you get wrong. In this example, testmakers bait you into fixating on the obvious comparison error, hoping that you will miss the subtler error of faulty predication. Also, they know that you are probably uncomfortable with the word "whereas" so they put it in answer choice E, counting on you not picking it because it sounds strange! **Remember: Focus on what you know to be wrong and eliminate all answer choices that contain concrete errors until you are left with one, whether you are comfortable with it or not.**

SKILLS MEET STRATEGY

Don't Forget About Logical Predication

If there is one grammar concept that people overlook on the GMAT and in their own writing, it is logical predication. The subject of a sentence must be logically linked to the predicate (verb and what follows the verb) or it is a meaning error called faulty predication. Consider this example: The organization believes that the new promotional campaign will raise donation levels by 50 percent. Would you notice the error of faulty predication in that sentence if you read it in a vacuum? Probably not, but an organization cannot believe (only people can believe). The key thing to remember on the GMAT is that you don't have to do this in a vacuum, but these errors can still be hard to notice, even with Decision Points to guide you.

SKILLBUILDER

- Comparisons
- Illogical meaning—faulty predication

3. Originally Charles City County, Virginia, natives, United States presidents William Henry Harrison and John Tyler share a unique place in American history: Harrison was the first president to die while in office, and Tyler was the first vice president promoted to succeed a deceased predecessor.

(A) Originally Charles City County, Virginia, natives, United States presidents William Henry Harrison and John Tyler share a unique place in American history

(B) Originally Charles City County, Virginia, natives, both United States presidents William Henry Harrison and John Tyler share unique places in American history

(C) United States presidents William Henry Harrison and John Tyler, both originally natives of Charles City County, Virginia, share a unique place in American history

(D) United States presidents William Henry Harrison and John Tyler, both natives of Charles City County, Virginia, share a unique place in American history

(E) Originally native to Charles City County, Virginia, United States presidents William Henry Harrison and John Tyler share a unique place in American history

LEARNING BY DOING
Redundant Constructions

While redundancy may not lead to a completely *illogical* meaning, it does create a ridiculous meaning and is at odds with the business goal of efficiency. Redundancy errors are very common on the GMAT (and in language in general!), so it is essential to look for this as a Decision Point. What is the redundancy in the question above? "Originally...natives." If you are a native, then you are necessarily originally from that place! The key, of course, is to notice this Decision Point and realize that only one of the answer choices correctly eliminates the redundant "originally." If you miss that Decision Point, then there are many unimportant differences that you might fixate on. Only answer choice D conveys the sentence properly and without redundancy.

SKILLS MEET STRATEGY
Redundancy Is Everywhere!

Do any of the common expressions from this list strike you as overkill?

- advance warning
- basic necessities
- ATM machine
- foreign import
- still remains
- unexpected surprise

When you start to notice redundancy, it becomes hard to stop—which is a good thing! Focusing on efficiency and meaning will help you to not only ace Sentence Correction on the GMAT but also improve your own writing. Redundancy is a *very* common error in language and is thus tested frequently on the GMAT.

SKILLBUILDER

- Illogical meaning—redundancy

Illogical Meaning: Quick Summary

Below is a quick summary of important takeaways for illogical meaning errors:

- Remember that many other error types will result in illogical meaning, but some errors are purely about logical and unambiguous meaning. These are highlighted below:

    1. Diction. **Make sure that the proper words are used to convey a meaning.**

    2. Faulty predication. **Make sure that the subject is logically linked to the verb and complete predicate that follows it.**

    3. Redundancy. **Make sure that the sentence does not contain a redundant structure.** Redundancy errors are common on the GMAT.

- **Meaning errors are often subtle and require careful analysis of the Decision Point differences.**

- Use logical meaning as your guide through most of Sentence Correction. It is the most important of the IMPACTS error types. Illogical meaning can be reviewed on pages 23–29 in the Skillbuilder.

Modifiers

If you understand the grammar rules for common modifiers, these errors are easy "low-hanging fruit" in the Decision Points process. Most modifier errors create distinct meaning problems, but you must know the rules to notice those problems. In other words, **make sure that you take the time to learn the grammatical rules relating to modifiers, as they are particularly important on the GMAT.** Before you look at several full modifier problems, let's review core rules from the Skillbuilder with the drills below:

MODIFIERS: CORE CONCEPTS FROM SKILLBUILDER

1. Prepositional phrases—These common modifiers need to be properly located in a sentence.

   Incorrect: ***Bill usually drops any groceries he has brought home from his job on the kitchen table.***

   Correct: ***Upon coming home from work, Bill usually drops any groceries on the kitchen table.***

2. Participial phrases—These -ing/-ed modifiers need to be beside the noun they are modifying (except in one important case that is frequently tested: when they are attached with a comma to the end of a clause or sentence).

   Incorrect: ***Alarmed by the recent decline of the stock market, many retirement investments have been switched from stocks to more conservative options, such as money market funds.***

   Correct: ***Alarmed by the recent decline of the stock market, many investors have switched their retirement investments from stocks to more conservative options, such as money market funds.***

3. Appositive phrases—Grammatically, these noun modifying phrases are treated nearly the same as participial phrases.

   Incorrect: ***A gifted student and talented musician, John's family was proud of him.***

   Correct: ***A gifted student and talented musician, John made his family proud.***

4. Relative clauses—These clauses are used to modify nouns only and in general must be beside the noun they are modifying (particularly with "which" clauses).

   Incorrect: ***It rained yesterday, which forced me to cancel the event.***

   Correct: ***It rained yesterday, and as a result I was forced to cancel the event.***

4. Published since 1851, the founders of the *New York Times* were Henry Jarvis Raymond and George Jones, who had no previous journalism experience.

   (A) Published since 1851, the founders of the *New York Times* were Henry Jarvis Raymond and George Jones, who had no previous journalism experience.

   (B) Published since 1851, Henry Jarvis Raymond and George Jones, who had no previous journalism experience, were the founders of the *New York Times.*

   (C) Published since 1851, the *New York Times* was founded by George Jones, who had no previous journalism experience, and Henry Jarvis Raymond.

   (D) The New York Times was founded by Henry Jarvis Raymond and George Jones, who had no previous journalism experience, and published since 1851.

   (E) The founders being Henry Jarvis Raymond and George Jones, who had no previous journalism experience, the *New York Times* has been published since 1851.

LEARNING BY DOING

Modifier Errors Are Easy to Spot

The glaring error in this question is the modifier at the beginning. "Published since 1851" cannot modify "the founders" or "Henry and George"; people are not published! This illogical construction dooms answer choices A and B, but it's remedied in answer choice C, the correct answer. Answer choices D and E both contain distinct sentence construction errors. In answer choice E, there is no active verb in the main clause; "being" is not a verb in that usage. The sentence in answer choice D leaves the "published since 1851" dangling at the end when it should be used as a modifier to start the sentence.

SKILLS MEET STRATEGY

Recognize Common Modifier Structures

Note the convenience of the modifier error in this example. After three words and the comma that follows them, you should have seen that a modifier was being tested. Many modifier errors occur at the beginning of a sentence, with a structure that involves a comma within or directly adjacent to the underlined portion:

_________________, fixed portion of the sentence → You need to select the modifier that logically describes the noun that follows.

Fixed modifier, _________________________ → You need to select the noun that can logically be described by the unchangeable modifier.

_________________________, _______________________ → When the entire construction is underlined, you need to select the answer choice that mixes and matches appropriately to find a legitimate combination of modifier and noun.

Many of the modifier errors you will see on the GMAT fit one of the three constructs above. If you recognize quickly that a modifier is being tested, you can eliminate multiple answer choices efficiently, without reading more than one-third of the sentence. You will then likely be left with another quick decision to make between the remaining choices.

As you have seen in the Skillbuilder, the GMAT primarily tests three categories of modifiers. A firm understanding of modifier errors allows you to make efficient work of many questions.

SKILLBUILDER

- Modifiers—participial phrase
- Sentence construction

5. The economic report released today by Congress and the Federal Reserve was bleaker than expected, which suggests that the nearing recession might be even deeper and more prolonged than even the most pessimistic analysts have predicted.

(A) which suggests that the nearing recession might be even deeper and more prolonged than even the most pessimistic analysts have predicted.

(B) which suggests that the nearing recession might be deeper and more prolonged than that predicted by even the most pessimistic analysts.

(C) suggests that the nearing recession might be even deeper and more prolonged than that predicted by even the most pessimistic analysts.

(D) suggesting that the nearing recession might be deeper and more prolonged than that predicted by even the most pessimistic analysts.

(E) a situation that is even more deep and prolonged than even the most pessimistic analysts have predicted.

LEARNING BY DOING

Participial Phrases and Relative Clauses

As you learned in the Skillbuilder, modifiers introduced by relative pronouns such as "which," "whose," or "where" have a simple rule: They must modify the noun (or noun phrase) that immediately precedes them. On the preceding page, answer choices A and B clearly violate this rule and are incorrect. A keen eye for relative clause errors can be instrumental in working through problems quickly and efficiently. Answer choice C is a textbook example of a comma splice error; you cannot write "the data was bleaker, suggests..." because there is no conjunction to link those clauses. Now that you are left with answer choices D and E, you should find the easy Decision Point relating to diction that many people miss: "deeper" vs. "more deep." Clearly, "more deep" is incorrect, and the correct answer choice is thus D.

SKILLS MEET STRATEGY

Know Certain Grammar Rules and Structures Well

Understanding common modifier structures and rules well is essential to success on the GMAT. As you will see shortly, you not only need to check modifiers for errors, but you also need to know when you can remove them from sentences to check for other core errors. There are two types of modifiers that people do not understand well and that are highlighted in the problem above: "which" clauses and "-ing" participial phrases. These are covered in detail in the Skillbuilder on pages 31–37, so make sure you take the time to understand these important structures well.

SKILLBUILDER

- Modifiers—participial phrases and relative clauses
- Sentence construction—comma splices
- Illogical meaning—diction

Modifiers: Quick Summary

As you've seen with modifier errors, the standard of usage comes down to logical agreement: Could the modifier logically describe the thing it is syntactically describing? **The simple rule of thumb is to put the modifier as close as possible to the noun it should describe, but you will see exceptions.** Make sure you are clear on the following strategy points:

- Modifier errors are generally easy to find, particularly if they are at the start of a sentence.
- **"Participial phrase" -ing modifiers can be used at the end of a sentence to modify the subject.** This is an important exception to the rule that modifiers should be as close as possible to what they are modifying.
- **The rules governing "which" clauses are strict**, but once you understand those rules, these errors are easy "low-hanging fruit" in the Decision Points process.
- Many modifiers, particularly appositive phrases, need to be removed to more clearly analyze the core structure of a sentence. (This "slash and burn" strategy will be covered shortly.)
- **The rules for modifiers are particularly important,** so take the time to review pages 22–31 of the Skillbuilder.

Pronouns

With pronoun errors, the focus shifts a bit from logical agreement to numerical agreement. Again, your clue comes in the Decision Points you encounter. If you see different pronouns (its/their; it/they; etc.) in the answer choices, you should be prepared to find the antecedent of the pronoun and decide whether it is singular or plural. Below is a summary of the important rules concerning agreement and reference with pronouns. Following that are several questions that test those two important concepts.

PRONOUNS: CORE CONCEPTS FROM SKILLBUILDER

1. Reference—A pronoun should clearly refer to a specific noun (its antecedent) in a sentence.

   Incorrect: ***Green and Holmes played, and he scored a touchdown.***

   Correct: ***Green and Holmes played, and Holmes scored a touchdown.***

2. Agreement—In addition to having a clear referent, pronouns must also agree in number with their antecedents (either singular or plural).

   Incorrect: ***The average mother expects unconditional love from her child, and they are rarely disappointed.***

   Correct: ***The average mother expects unconditional love from her child, and she is rarely disappointed.***

6. The company manual specifically outlines rules for employees about contacting managers while they are out of the office on vacation or for personal reasons.

(A) for employees about contacting managers while they are out of the office on vacation or for personal reasons

(B) for employees about contacting their managers out of the office on vacation or for personal reasons

(C) for employees about contacting managers who are out of the office on vacation or for personal reasons

(D) for employees about contacting managers who are out of their office on vacation or for personal reasons

(E) for employees about contacting managers if they are out of their office on vacation or for personal reasons

7. Even today, <u>lions can be seen ruling the African plains</u>, hunting almost any animal that crosses its path and intimidating all but the most intrepid hunters.

(A) lions can be seen ruling the African plains

(B) lions are able to be seen ruling the African plains

(C) lions rule the African plains

(D) the lion rules the African plains

(E) the lion species rules the African plains

LEARNING BY DOING

Pronoun Reference and Pronoun Agreement

The two previous questions contain tricky examples of the core pronoun error types: reference and agreement. The first problem (#6) is about reference. If there is a pronoun in a sentence, it must be crystal clear to whom or what that pronoun is referring. In answer choice A, it is unclear to whom "they" is referring; does the rule apply when the managers are out of the office or when the employees are out of the office? The same error exists in answer choice E, so both can be eliminated. In answer choice D, the possessive pronoun "their" also creates a reference error: Is the sentence referring to the managers' offices or the employees' offices? In answer choice B, there is not a pronoun error, but the meaning of the sentence is still unclear concerning when the rule applies (as it was in answer choices A and E). Only answer choice C, the correct answer, eliminates the pronoun problems and makes the meaning clear and logical.

In the second question (#7), you see a slight twist on the traditional pronoun agreement error. Instead of having to pick the correct pronoun, you have to pick the correct antecedent to match a pronoun. You're stuck with "its" as the pronoun, so as much as you'd like to use the plural form "lions," you simply cannot, as the antecedent must be singular. This allows you to eliminate answer choices A, B, and C. Then you must notice the tricky meaning error in answer choice E: the use of "species" creates an illogical meaning with "any animal crossing its path." Animals don't cross a species' path, but rather a particular animal's path. Answer choice E is wrong because of a subtle meaning error that is easy to miss. The correct answer choice is D.

SKILLS MEET STRATEGY

Recognize Common Pronoun Tricks

It is difficult for testmakers to make pronoun error problems hard, but when they do, they typically use the same set-ups over and over. For agreement, that set-up is fixing the pronoun outside of the underlined portion and making you pick the proper antecedent. **Make sure that you always take note of pronouns, whether they are in the underlined portion or not.** Reference errors are subtler and more difficult overall, so you will see them more often in tricky pronoun problems. The important thing to remember for these problems is that **reference errors are often corrected by simply eliminating any unclear pronouns from the sentence.**

SKILLS MEET STRATEGY

Assess Pronoun Errors First

Pronoun errors are rarely difficult, and as a result, you should assess them first. **Any time that you see a pronoun within the sentence (underlined or not), it is the first Decision Point you should assess.** Ask yourself the following two questions: Is the pronoun (or the antecedent) supposed to be singular or plural, and is it crystal clear to whom or what the pronoun is referring? **Pronoun errors are "low-hanging fruit," but they are also easy to miss, so keep your eyes peeled for pronouns in every Sentence Correction problem.**

SKILLBUILDER

- Pronoun—agreement
- Pronoun—reference
- Illogical meaning

8. John was one of the few people to get his hands on an advance ticket for U2's North American tour—a tour that was delayed by several months on account of front man Bono's back injury.

   (A) to get his hands on an advance ticket for U2's North American tour—a tour that was delayed by several months on account of front man Bono's back injury

   (B) to get their hands on an advance ticket for U2's North American tour—a tour that was delayed by several months due to front man Bono and his back injury

   (C) to get their hands on an advance ticket for U2's North American tour—a tour that was delayed by several months because of front man Bono's back injury

   (D) who got his hands on an advance ticket for U2's North American tour—a tour that was delayed by several months on account of front man Bono and his back injury

   (E) who got his hands on an advance ticket for U2's North American tour—a tour that was delayed because of front man Bono and his back injury

LEARNING BY DOING

Find the Correct Antecedent

The trickiest pronoun problems are ones in which it is difficult to determine to whom or what the pronoun is referring (not a reference error, but rather a confusing structure). This confusion usually comes when modifiers are involved, as is the case with this problem. Before you tackle that issue on this problem, you should first find the easiest Decision Points. At the end there is an obvious and relatively easy choice between "Bono's back injury" and "Bono and his back injury." The tour was not canceled because of Bono and then separately his back injury, so that is a classic error of diction. You can safely eliminate answer choices B, D, and E. In the choice between answer choices A and C, the most important Decision Point is the "his" vs. "their." Ask yourself what the modifying infinitive phrase "to get their hands on" is really modifying; the answer is people. What kind of people? People to get their hands on.... It is easy to think that John is the antecedent and pick answer choice A, but the correct answer choice is C. Also, you should note that there are Decision Points involving "because" vs. "due to" vs. "on account of" in this problem. If you are answering the question why in any sentence, remember that you should use the word "because" (or accepted synonyms such as "for" and "since"), not "due to" or "on account of."

SKILLS MEET STRATEGY

Use Logic!

Focusing on logical meaning can help you avoid mistakes on a problem like this. If you casually approach the pronoun without considering meaning, it would be easy to erroneously pick the singular pronoun "his," thinking it refers to the obvious noun in the sentence ("John"). However, if you go through the thought process outlined in the explanation and really ask what makes sense, it is clear that the modifier is referring to people and the pronoun must be plural.

SKILLBUILDER

- Pronoun—agreement
- Illogical meaning—diction

Pronouns: Quick Summary

Pronoun errors are generally straightforward, but they can be difficult and/or easy to miss when presented in particular structures. For pronoun errors, remember the following:

- **Assess pronoun errors first.** If there is a pronoun anywhere in the sentence, take note of it and search for any relevant Decision Points. Most pronoun errors are easy to understand.
- Pronoun agreement errors are easy to miss when the pronoun is placed outside of the underlined portion. **REMEMBER: In agreement problems, you may need to change the antecedent to get proper agreement.**
- Reference errors are subtler and harder to recognize. **Remember that many reference errors are corrected by simply removing the pronoun(s) altogether.**
- Pronoun errors can be particularly tricky in certain modifier structures. If you are confused about what noun a pronoun is referring to, use logic to assess the meaning.
- Pronoun errors can be reviewed on pages 43–45 in the Skillbuilder.

Agreement *(Between Subject and Verb)*

Similar to pronoun errors, agreement errors hinge on your ability to recognize singular vs. plural subjects and match them to their respective counterparts, in this case verbs. Below is a summary of common errors relating to agreement. That is followed by several problems and an important summary of one of the most important strategies in sentence correction: "slash and burn."

AGREEMENT: CORE CONCEPTS FROM SKILLBUILDER

There are four common set-ups in which assessing subject-verb agreement is difficult:

1. When the subject is very far away from the verb that it is commanding

   Incorrect: ***The number of applicants to the top business schools are increasing every year.***

   Correct: ***The number of applicants to the top business schools is increasing every year.***

2. When the subject is in the form "x or y," "either x or y," or "neither x nor y"

   Incorrect: ***Neither John nor his friends is going to the movies.***

   Correct: ***Neither John nor his friends are going to the movies.***

3. When the verb comes before the subject

   Incorrect: ***Sitting at the far end of the bar is a local television reporter and one of the town's leading candidates for mayor.***

   Correct: ***Sitting at the far end of the bar are a local television reporter and one of the town's leading candidates for mayor.***

4. When confusing or unusual nouns/subjects are used

   Incorrect: ***A thousand dollars are a lot of money.***

   Correct: ***A thousand dollars is a lot of money.***

9. The quality of the new products that ACME Corporation have developed over the past year and that have recently arrived on retailers' shelves worry many business analysts, who think that the company has lost focus under the new CEO's leadership.

(A) The quality of the new products that ACME Corporation have developed over the past year and that have recently arrived on retailers' shelves worry

(B) The quality of the new products that ACME Corporation has developed over the past year and that has recently arrived on retailers' shelves worry

(C) The quality of the new products that ACME Corporation have developed over the past year and that has recently arrived on retailers' shelves worry

(D) The quality of the new products that ACME Corporation has developed over the past year and that have recently arrived on retailers' shelves worries

(E) The quality of the new products that ACME Corporation have developed over the past year and that have recently arrived on retailers' shelves worries

LEARNING BY DOING

Find the Proper Subject

This question is a classic example of the agreement (between subject and verb) error family. Note the telltale signs:

- A 3-2 split between the singular and plural forms of the same verb ("worry" in A/B/C vs. "worries" in D/E)
- Prepositional phrases to fill the sentence with several nouns, obscuring the true subject of the sentence

With agreement questions, once you have noticed one (or both) of these signals, your job becomes to identify the subject of the verb in question. Two strategies will help you in that pursuit: slash and burn (get rid of all unnecessary sentence elements) and logic. The most obvious Decision Point on the problem above is "worry" vs. "worries"; decide using slash and burn (and logic) what the subject is. By getting rid of all the modifiers, it is clear that "quality" is the subject for that verb *and* it makes sense (quality can logically worry), so answer choices A, B, and C are wrong. In your choice between answer choices D and E, there is only one Decision Point: "has developed" vs. "have developed." Since the corporation is the subject (logically and grammatically) for that verb, it must be the singular "has developed." Answer choice D is correct.

SKILLS MEET STRATEGY

Don't Forget About Logical Meaning

If you are struggling to get rid of modifiers and figure out the proper subject, don't forget about logic. What really "worries many business analysts" here? The closest noun is "retailers' shelves," but that doesn't seem logical. Neither does "the past year" or "ACME Corporation." It's the dubious quality of the new products. **Often you can make these decisions by logically determining which noun has the capacity to perform the verb in question, even if you are struggling with slash and burn.**

SKILLS MEET STRATEGY

Slash and Burn

As described in detail on the next page, the slash-and-burn strategy works not only on agreement-based questions but also on a variety of other error-type questions. The GMAT often employs the "weapon of mass distraction" by turning a short, efficient sentence into a long, unwieldy one through the use of adjectives, adverbs, modifiers, and independent clauses. Eliminating clutter in each sentence can help you to reduce the amount that you read, and, as you do so, the errors should become much more apparent. **After Decision Points, the slash-and-burn strategy is *the* most important ingredient for success in sentence correction.**

SKILLBUILDER

- Subject-verb agreement

Slash and Burn

By "overstuffing" sentences, testmakers can confuse people about which noun(s) is (are) the subject(s), or which words in a sentence are actionable (or even necessary).

To combat this tactic, test-takers should learn to ignore descriptive terms (adjectives, adverbs, and modifying phrases that are not part of a modifier error; discussed in the next section) and to identify which clauses of a sentence can similarly be ignored as being irrelevant to the underlined portion of a sentence.

Consider the previous sentence in more detail using this important technique:

> *The quality of the new products that ACME Corporation have developed over the past year and that have recently arrived on retailers' shelves worry many business analysts, who think that the company has lost focus under the new CEO's leadership.*

First, eliminate modifying phrases.

> *The quality ~~of the new products~~ ~~that ACME Corporation have developed~~ ~~over the past year~~ ~~and that have recently arrived~~ ~~on retailers' shelves~~ worry many business analysts, ~~who think that the company has lost focus under the new CEO's leadership~~.*

"Of the new products" just tells us "which quality?" And "that ACME Corporation have developed" and "that have recently arrived" tell us more about "the products."

"Over the past year" and "on retailers' shelves" modify "developed" and "arrived," respectively.

And "who think..." tells us more about "analysts." Without those modifying clauses we're left with simply:

> *The quality worry many business analysts.*

Then, as necessary, eliminate adjectives and adverbs.

Here there are only two, and you may well notice the glaring error even without eliminating them. But "some" and "business" exist only to describe "analysts," so for our consideration of subject-verb agreement they are simply in the way. Eliminating them leaves us with just:

> *The quality worry analysts.*

And clearly that commits a major subject-verb agreement error, and the correct verb should be "worries."

Slash and Burn—But You Can Still Recycle

Now, notice that the strategy allows you to "put back" phrases that are actually necessary to your Decision Points. The next decision to be made was between "have developed" and "has developed," so you'll want to keep those phrases in the sentence for the next decision:

> *The quality of the products that ACME Corporation have developed worries (we've already corrected this) analysts.*

Because "ACME have developed" is wrong, we can now make that final decision.

Use It or Lose It Modifier Strategy

As you know, modifier errors are another common GMAT Decision Point. To employ the slash-and-burn strategy most effectively, think of modifiers with the phrase "use it or lose it."

When you see a modifying phrase, either "use it" as a Decision Point to eliminate the answer choice or, if it's correctly used, then "lose it"—that is, eliminate it via slash and burn so that it's out of the way and you can focus on the rest of the sentence to find errors.

When applicable, break off irrelevant clauses. The previous sentence did not include one, but others will. Consider the sentence (an excerpt from one of your homework questions):

> *A recent research study of worldwide cellular penetration finds that there are now one mobile phone for every two people, more than twice as many than there were in 2005.*

The clause "A recent research study finds that" exists to set up the dependent clause "there are now one mobile phone." As that clause has no bearing on the Decision Points in this question, you can break off that introductory clause to shorten the sentence:

> *There are now one mobile phone for every two people, more than twice as many than there were in 2005.*

Now that the introductory clause is gone, you can further streamline the sentence by eliminating modifiers:

> *There are now one mobile phone ~~for every two people~~, ~~more than twice as many than there were in 2005.~~*

And eliminate adjectives and adverbs:

> *There are ~~now one mobile~~ phone.*

You find a glaring subject-verb agreement error in the sentence: "There are phone."

In summary, to efficiently slash and burn, you should:

1. Eliminate modifiers.

   "Use it or lose it." If a modifier isn't used as your Decision Point to eliminate the answer choice, then slash and burn it.

2. Break off irrelevant clauses.

3. Eliminate adjectives and adverbs.

   Slash and burn—but you can still recycle.

Slash and Burn Drill

Using slash and burn to assess Sentence Correction problems can make your reading of these sentences exponentially more efficient. This skill takes practice, but as you work through problems you will see the payoffs as you quickly hone in on errors and you save energy for later problems. **In this drill, "eliminate the clutter" (all prepositional phrases, modifying phrases, and other modifiers if they bother you), identify each subject, and correct any verbs that don't agree with what their subjects dictate.**

1. Under the provisions of the Internal Revenue Code, a 501(c)(3) organization, retaining a unique designation among American tax-exempt nonprofits, are permitted to conduct voter-education activities provided these activities remain non-partisan.

2. The damage caused by the series of storms were relatively minimal, but among the casualties were a cluster of farmhouses on the western outskirts of the town.

3. Though the origin of the terms "bull market" and "bear market," which refer to upward and downward market trends, respectively, are debated, these colloquialisms have been hallmarks of financial parlance for more than a century.

Slash and Burn Solutions

1. ~~Under the provisions of the Internal Revenue Code,~~ a 501(c)(3) organization, ~~retaining a unique designation among American tax-exempt nonprofits,~~ IS permitted to conduct voter-education activities provided these activities remain non-partisan.

2. The damage caused ~~by the series of storms~~ WAS relatively minimal, but ~~among the casualties~~ WAS a cluster ~~of farmhouses on the western outskirts of the town~~.

3. Though the origin ~~of the terms "bull market" and "bear market", which refer to upward and downward market trends, respectively~~, IS debated, these colloquialisms have been hallmarks ~~of financial parlance for more than a century~~.

Agreement: Another Twist

has

10. Out of a growing pride in the region's pre-automotive achievements have developed a committee for the preservation of Detroit's landmarks and artifacts that are creating monuments and museums across the city.

    (A) have developed a committee for the preservation of Detroit's landmarks and artifacts that are creating

    (B) has developed a committee for the preservation of Detroit's landmarks and artifacts that is creating

    (C) has developed a committee for the preservation of Detroit's landmarks and artifacts that create

    (D) have developed a committee for the preservation of Detroit's landmarks and artifacts that creates

    (E) have developed a committee for the preservation of Detroit's landmarks and artifacts that create

LEARNING BY DOING
Subject-Verb Inversion

This question highlights another clever GMAT tactic to throw you off the scent of subject-verb agreement: It inverts the subject and verb. "...has developed a committee" is akin to saying "so am I" instead of "I am, also." Stylistically, many constructions allow for the subject to follow the verb. In this case, recognize that both logic and modifier elimination should direct you to the true subject.

"Out of a growing pride" leads with a preposition ("out of") and therefore functions as a modifying phrase. It describes why the committee has developed. You could just as easily flip the sentence around:

A committee has developed out of a growing pride in the region's pre-automotive achievements....

So the main subject in this sentence is "a committee." This allows you to eliminate answer choices A, D, and E, as you cannot say "a committee have developed...." For answer choices B and C, the only remaining decision point is between "create," which is a plural verb in the present tense, and "is creating," which is a singular verb in the present continuous tense. To make that decision, you must decide what noun is commanding that verb and whether it is singular. The best way to answer that question is with simple logic. What is doing the creating? The committee. Since committee is singular, the correct answer choice is B, which contains the proper "is creating."

THINK LIKE THE TESTMAKER

Misdirection and Hiding the Correct Answer

As you do more and more Sentence Correction problems, you will see repeating patterns for how testmakers make them hard: They insert lots of confusing modifiers, they construct complex sentences with multiple clauses, and they invert the subject and the verb. Subject-verb inversion can serve multiple purposes in making questions difficult. It makes it hard to find the correct subject, but it also creates awkward-sounding sentences that people are hesitant to pick (even though they are correct). Don't let subject-verb inversion lead you astray in finding the proper subject, and don't let it keep you from picking the correct answer just because it sounds strange to your ear.

SKILLS MEET STRATEGY

Embrace Subject-Verb Inversion

Make sure you understand that, while subject-verb inversion is a common GMAT device to trap you, it is also a common way of phrasing sentences that you use every day. Think of the "there is..." construction used in so many sentences:

- *There's something about Mary.*
- *There are 50 ways to leave your lover.*

While often the GMAT uses subject-verb inversion structures that sound a bit off to your ear, those structures are valid and correct. Know this about inversion: It is often necessary in order to avoid a misplaced or ambiguous modifier, but sometimes it is just stylistic. Subject-verb inversion is, to a large extent, a nice trick up the GMAT authors' sleeves, but it is also a very normal function of speech and one that you use every day. Do not fear it, but do learn to recognize it.

SKILLBUILDER

- Subject-verb agreement

Agreement: Quick Summary

When distilled into its pure form, subject-verb agreement is actually quite simple: If the subject is singular, the verb should be singular; if the subject is plural, the verb should be plural. In reality, it is much more confusing than that, because the subject can be hard to locate in complicated structures. Make sure to keep the following in mind when assessing agreement errors:

- **Use the slash-and-burn technique to get rid of all modifiers when assessing subject-verb agreement.** Remember: If a noun is the object of a modifying phrase, it cannot be the subject of the sentence.
- Many subjects will be very far away from the verb that they command.
- **If you are still confused about the subject after employing slash and burn, make sure you think about the relationship logically.** People forget about logical meaning (logical predication) when assessing subject-verb agreement. Ask yourself if the noun can logically command the verb that you are considering.
- **Subject-verb inversion in a sentence makes the subject particularly difficult to find.** Remember that the subject can come after the verb it is commanding.
- Sometimes a verb does not agree grammatically with the noun that commands it. (A thousand dollars is a lot of money!)
- Subject-verb agreement can be reviewed on pages 49–54 in the Skillbuilder.

Comparisons

Comparison errors are particularly difficult and require a degree of precision not seen in other error types. When you see comparison structures, focus your attention specifically on the nature of the comparison. Make your mantra "What is being compared?" If you can do that precisely (which is admittedly difficult on the hardest questions) you will answer these questions correctly. Below is a review of the core concepts relating to comparison errors followed by two tricky comparison questions:

COMPARISONS: CORE CONCEPTS FROM SKILLBUILDER

1. Comparisons must be logical in what they compare.

   Incorrect: ***Group A's findings are more significant than Group B.***

   Correct: ***Group A's findings are more significant than those of Group B.***

   Incorrect: ***Software X crashes more often than Software J.***

   Correct: ***Software X crashes more often than does Software J.***

2. In a comparison, the grammatical form of each component should be equivalent.

   Incorrect: ***To imitate someone's success is not the same as duplicating it.***

   Correct: ***Imitating someone's success is not the same as duplicating it.***

11. Known to its considerable opposition as "Seward's Folly," the purchase of Alaska was <u>not unlike that of the Louisiana territory, which provided</u> the United States with new land, a strategic military position, and control of the entire Mississippi River valley.

    (A) not unlike that of the Louisiana territory, which provided

    (B) not unlike the Louisiana territory, which provided

    (C) like the Louisiana territory, which provided

    (D) like that of the Louisiana territory for providing

    (E) as that of the Louisiana territory for providing

LEARNING BY DOING

Avoid Apples-to-Oranges Comparisons

When you first examine this question, there are several clear Decision Points: "not unlike" vs. "like" vs. "as" *and* "which provided" vs. "for providing." The easiest Decision Point, however, is a little harder to notice: the choice between having "that of" and not having it. To make this a logical, apples-to-apples comparison you must have "that of"—are you comparing the **purchase** of Alaska to "**Louisiana**" or "**that** of (meaning the **purchase** of) Louisiana"? "That of Louisiana" is necessary to make it a logical, purchase-to-purchase comparison, so answer choices B and C are incorrect. Also, answer choice E is incorrect, because you do not use "as" to make noun-to-noun comparisons (but you will be able to eliminate it for other reasons as well). Importantly, the choice between "like" and "not unlike" is a classic false Decision Point; they could both be used here, but people often eliminate "not unlike" prematurely.

The remaining decision is more difficult and quite subtle, but you should at least know to assess it because of the obvious Decision Point. As you have seen in earlier examples, you will often want to scan the answer choices at the first and last words/phrases for differences, and here there is a 2-1 split between "territory, which provided" and "territory for providing." What is the difference? "Which provided" makes it clear that the Louisiana territory provided the new land, strategic position, and Mississippi River valley. "For providing" leaves that ambiguous at best, or assigns it to Alaska at worst. Either way, the meaning is either unclear or incorrect, and answer choices D and E suffer from this modifier reference problem. Answer choice A—the choice that many eliminate upon first glance for the double-negative—is correct.

THINK LIKE THE TESTMAKER

Hiding the Correct Answer

Subject-verb inversion (which you saw in the "Agreement" section) is a tactic that GMAT testmakers often employ to add awkwardness and obfuscate the correct answer. The double negative "not unlike" in this problem is another great example of how testmakers put something in the correct answer to keep you from picking it. People hate the double negative, but it's not incorrect (look, there it is again!). "Not unlike" means "it's not wholly different; there's at least some similarity there," whereas "like" means "quite similar to." Each has its own meaning, so the double negative is functional here. **As an astute GMAT test-taker, you should look for a proper comparison before you try to make decisions based on style. "Not unlike" is the GMAT's lure to draw your attention away from the important decision. Don't let the testmakers bait you into considering false Decision Points or avoiding a correct answer just because it sounds weird or contains an unusual structure.**

SKILLS MEET STRATEGY

Recognize Comparison Trigger Words

"That of" is a construction you should get used to seeing in answer choices as a Decision Point. If you see the construction "that of" or "those of," there's a high likelihood you're being asked to decide how to render a proper comparison. Here are some other important comparison trigger words:

- **As many as/as much as**
- **More than/less than/-er than**
- **Like/unlike**
- **Similar to/different from**

When you see any of these words, your comparison antennae should go up, and you should make sure that the answer you pick is making a proper and precise comparison.

SKILLS MEET STRATEGY

Focus on Core Competencies

This problem is a great one for emphasizing the strategies presented at the start of this lesson. **In Sentence Correction, the testmakers will often bait you into making decisions that you are not qualified to make (and that you don't have to make!).** The key in using the Decision Points strategy is to make sure you leverage all choices and consider carefully which ones to start with. There are many decisions in Sentence Correction that you should never try to make. Just because you are given choices, it does not mean they matter or that you must make a choice. **If you are unsure of a decision, leave it alone and move to another, hopefully easier, Decision Point**.

SKILLBUILDER

- Comparisons
- Modifiers
- Logical meaning—diction

12. In order to ensure that chemical reactions in the lab behave as predicted by their mathematical formulas, it is important that heat be applied evenly over the total surface area of the flask instead of a series of irregular points on its surface.

(A) instead of

(B) as compared with

(C) in contrast with

(D) rather than to

(E) as against being at

LEARNING BY DOING

Comparisons Must Be Equivalent in Form

As you can see from this problem, it is critical to determine precisely what is being compared. What is being compared in this sentence? ***Where*** the heat is being applied. If you said "location," you're partially correct, but with a significant piece missing. In the first portion of the comparison, the heat is being applied "over the total surface area." Yes, "the total surface area" is the location of the application, but the word "over" is just as important. Without a preposition to introduce the location in the second portion of the comparison ("to a series of irregular points"), the comparison lacks equivalency of form. To be properly compared, the heat must be applied evenly:

1. ***over*** the entire surface area

   rather than

2. ***to*** a series of irregular points.

None of the other answer choices (except answer choice E, which is clearly wrong because of the poor diction ("as against being") contain the necessary preposition of location to make an exact comparison between the same things: **where** the heat is being applied. The correct answer choice is D.

SKILLS MEET STRATEGY

Always Ask Yourself What Is Being Compared

Remember that comparisons need to be incredibly precise. They must be both logical (apples-to-apples comparisons) and equivalent in form (i.e., parallel). To determine if you have met those criteria, always start comparison problems by answering the following question precisely: What is being compared? In this example, if you answered "the location," you can see how you would probably get it wrong. But if you answer "where the heat is being applied," you will notice the importance of the preposition of location and go straight to answer choice D.

SKILLBUILDER

- Comparisons

Comparisons: Quick Summary

As you can see from this example, comparison problems on the GMAT require a real precision, and thus you will often have to spend a bit more time than you would on other questions. To succeed on these questions, remember the following:

- Most comparison problems contain common trigger words that help you recognize this error type.
- **Comparisons need to be logical. Make sure that you are comparing nouns logically, and make sure you avoid noun-to-action comparisons.**
- **Comparisons need to be equivalent in form.** If the comparison is logical but lacks equivalency, it is still incorrect.
- Comparison error problems are often the most difficult on the GMAT. Take extra time to unlock the comparison and make sure it is perfectly precise. They can be reviewed on pages 57–64 in the Skillbuilder.

Tense

Tense errors occur when a sentence creates an illogical time line. Your standard of decision-making when it comes to time line–based questions is that the verbs should connote a **logical** time line. Before moving to some drills and questions, let's first review some core skills from the Skillbuilder:

TENSE: CORE CONCEPTS FROM SKILLBUILDER

1. Understand the different tenses, particularly the past perfect.

   Incorrect: ***After meeting with Bill, John realized that he forgot to give him the proposal.***

   Correct: ***After meeting with Bill, John realized that he had forgotten to give him the proposal.***

2. Understand subjunctive mood and passive voice (verb form, not verb tense).

   Incorrect: ***In a school meeting, the principal demanded that students are quiet in class or face the consequences.***

   Correct: ***In a school meeting, the principal demanded that students be quiet in class or face the consequences.***

Now decide which of the following sentences are correct from a tense perspective:

My grandfather was a carpenter until the day he died.

My grandfather had been a carpenter for 55 years by the time he died.

Having been a carpenter his entire adult life, my grandfather died in a house he had built himself.

In the triathlon, I swam 2.4 miles, biked 112 miles, and then ran a full marathon.

In the triathlon, I had already swum 2.4 miles and biked 112 miles before I even started the full marathon.

Surprise—they all are! Even though the five sentences use an array of verb tenses to connote the same events (grandfather was a carpenter, grandfather died; I swam, I biked, I ran), each is used appropriately. As you approach time line–based questions, recognize that there is not always one necessary verb tense, but rather a handful of verb forms that can convey the proper time line in combination with other expressions and words. **Many test-takers find themselves searching for "the perfect" verb tense and accordingly eliminating valid answer choices. If a time line is logical, you've done your job with verb tenses, and you'll need to find another Decision Point.**

13. Some of the homes that were destroyed and structurally compromised in the fire last year had been built by the community's earliest settlers.

    (A) Some of the homes that were destroyed and structurally compromised in the fire last year had been

    (B) Some of the homes that were destroyed or structurally compromised in the fire last year had been

    (C) Some of the homes that the fire destroyed and structurally compromised last year have been

    (D) Last year the fire destroyed or structurally compromised some of the homes that have been

    (E) Last year some of the homes that were destroyed or structurally compromised in the fire had been

LEARNING BY DOING

Keep Track of the Time Line

In this problem, notice the function of the phrase "Last year" to set up a time line. It is illogical that, all in the last year, the earliest settlers to the community built houses *and* those houses were subsequently destroyed in a fire. Answer choices D and E, just by leading with that entire-sentence modifier "Last year," begin to fail the logical time line test. And answer choices C and D both use the ongoing tense "have been," putting the building of the homes (by early settlers, nonetheless) *after* the fire that burned them down! That time line is even more nonsensical. Only answer choices A and B construct a logical time line using the phrasing:

The homes *were* ruined in the fire ***and*** the homes *had been* built by early settlers.

So what's the difference? Verb tense conveys meaning but so do conjunctions (more to come on this in the Sentence Construction section!). Does it make sense to say that a home can be both destroyed and structurally compromised? If it is destroyed, then it is necessarily compromised, so the conjunction must be "or." The correct answer choice is B.

SKILLS MEET STRATEGY

Don't Ignore Small Decision Points

The problem with Decision Points between small words such as pronouns and conjunctions is that they are easy to miss. If you use good strategy on a problem like this, you should narrow down to answer choices A and B and then realize that the only difference between them is the choice of "and" vs. "or." That may not seem like an important choice in your first read-through (or you may miss it altogether), but the whole problem hinges on the important meaning difference between those two conjunctions. While people tend to use conjunctions loosely in their own writing, these important sentence elements are tested with a high level of precision on the GMAT.

SKILLBUILDER

- Tense
- Sentence construction—conjunctions

14. A 1999 tax bill <u>changed what many wealthy taxpayers and large corporations are allowed to deduct on their tax returns</u>.

    (A) changed what many wealthy taxpayers and large corporations are allowed to deduct on their tax returns

    (B) changed wealthy taxpayers' and large corporations' amounts that they have been allowed to deduct on their tax returns

    (C) is changing wealthy taxpayers' and large corporations' amounts that they have been allowed to deduct on their tax returns

    (D) changed what many wealthy taxpayers and large corporations had been allowed to deduct on their tax returns

    (E) changes what many wealthy taxpayers and large corporations have been allowed to deduct on their tax returns

LEARNING BY DOING

Verb Tense Can Be Confusing

This difficult problem captures how important the concept of "logical time lines" is when considering tense (and the past perfect in particular). The easiest decision point to start with in this problem is the tense of the verb "to change" at the beginning of each answer choice. Since 1999 is in the past, the verb must be "changed"; you can safely eliminate answer choices C and E. Also, the improper diction in "taxpayers' and corporations' amounts" is incorrect in answer choice B, so it is relatively easy to get the problem down to two choices: A and D. To determine which one is correct you must think logically: Can a tax bill enacted in 1999 affect what you are allowed to deduct today? Yes! Can a tax bill enacted in 1999 affect what you were allowed to deduct before 1999? No! Answer choice D illogically suggests that the bill changed what people could do before the bill was passed, and that is simply not possible. Even though it might sound a little strange when you first read it, answer choice A is correct. In 1999 a tax bill changed what everyone is allowed to do today.

SKILLS MEET STRATEGY

Use Logic over "Grammar"

This problem is difficult regardless of how you approach it. The meaning issue created by the past perfect is subtle, and answer choice D might sound better to your ear than answer choice A. The only way that you will get this correct is if you have a primary focus on logical meaning. Remember: Grammar exists mainly to create a framework for clarity and efficiency. Don't just try to memorize a set of disconnected grammar rules, but instead focus on what makes sense and what is logical.

SKILLBUILDER

- Tense
- Illogical meaning—diction

15. While the nurses frantically searched for his parents to collect his vital information, the injured boy calmly explained to the doctor that his blood type was O positive.

    (A) the injured boy calmly explained to the doctor that his blood type was O positive

    (B) the injured boy had calmly explained to the doctor that his blood type was O positive

    (C) the boy was injured and explained that his blood type is O positive to the doctor

    (D) the boy, who was injured, calmly explained to the doctor that his blood type was O positive

    (E) the injured boy calmly explained to the doctor that his blood type is O positive

LEARNING BY DOING

Use the Present Tense in Universal Statements

Like the last problem, this one highlights the importance of logic in analyzing tense. It also highlights a rule you should remember going forward: If something universal is being described (i.e., something that does not change) then you should use the present tense, regardless of the time line or accompanying tenses. To attack this problem, you should first eliminate answer choices B, C, and D. In answer choice B, the past perfect is wrong because of the word "while" to start the sentence; this is all happening at one point in the past. Answer choice C suggests illogically that the boy was injured while the nurses searched for his parents, and answer choice D uses the awkward and unnecessary relative clause "boy, who was injured" instead of "injured boy." For the choice between answer choices A and E, the only difference is "was" vs. "is." Because everything in this sentence is in the past tense, it would be easy to pick answer choice A to match that tense. But think about answer choice A logically: If he told the doctor that his blood type was O positive, then that suggests illogically that it is now somehow different. Blood types don't ever change! If you are ever describing something universal such as this, the present tense (in this case "is") must be used, so answer choice E is correct.

THINK LIKE THE TESTMAKER

Misdirection

What makes this problem hard? You are "set up" to fail by the testmakers! In most of the problems you have done so far, if you insert the present tense with the past tense it would create an illogical and incorrect sentence. So what do the testmakers do? They find an important exception and bait you with it. Remember: While you could try to learn all these exceptions, you don't *have* to do that (and it is an incredibly inefficient way to prepare). If you simply thought about the logic and the meaning differences between "is" and "was" you could reason out this exception on your own. As you have seen clearly in this section on tense, logic (not rules!) should be your guide through sentence correction.

SKILLBUILDER

- Tense
- Modifiers

Tense: Quick Summary

Clearly, tense errors can be difficult, but by using logical time lines and a basic understanding of the different tenses, you can get even the most difficult problems correct. Make sure you focus on the following:

- **There are many different ways to express a time line within a sentence.** Be flexible with tense, and focus on whether the tenses and accompanying time phrases are logical. **Use the concept of "logical time lines" as your guide in any problem with tense Decision Points.**
- **Understand the past perfect well.** It is commonly tested tense in harder problems and is a confusing tense for many students.
- Remember to use the present tense for universal statements.
- You can review the different tenses with drills and explanations on pages 67–71 in the Skillbuilder.

Sentence Construction

Sentence construction errors take three forms: punctuation and linking clauses; parallelism in series; and parallelism in common structures. GMAT problems that feature sentence construction errors are often viewed as difficult, in large part because finding the appropriate linking clause and preposition Decision Points is akin to finding a needle in a haystack. Moreover, these problems tend to feature longer-than-average underlined portions, again making Decision Points harder to find. **On these problems, your use of the slash-and-burn technique will be essential in helping to isolate these decisions.** Below is a review of core concepts relating to sentence construction errors followed by two problems:

SENTENCE CONSTRUCTION: CORE CONCEPTS FROM SKILLBUILDER

1. Sentence construction errors relating to punctuation and linking clauses

   Incorrect: ***Being unemployed can be difficult for anyone but John was having a particularly hard time with it.***

   Correct: ***Being unemployed can be difficult for anyone, but John was having a particularly hard time with it.***

2. Sentence construction errors relating to parallelism in a series

   Incorrect: ***At summer camp, Johnny likes basketball, tennis, and to play soccer.***

   Correct: ***At summer camp, Johnny likes basketball, tennis, and soccer.***

3. Sentence construction errors relating to parallelism in common constructions such as not only/but also, either/or, etc.

   Incorrect: ***John will either win a million dollars on the game show tomorrow or he will walk away with nothing.***

   Correct: ***John will either win a million dollars on the game show tomorrow or walk away with nothing.***

16. The increase in the number of American households viewing telecasts of NASCAR races imply that the motorsport will soon supplant NFL football as the nation's most popular sport, but that the limited number of races each year compared to the NFL's hundreds of games indicates that fans will continue to watch football at a significantly higher rate.

    (A) imply that the motorsport will soon supplant NFL football as the nation's most popular sport, but that

    (B) imply that the motorsport is soon supplanting NFL football as the nation's most popular sport, but

    (C) implies that the motorsport will soon supplant NFL football as the nation's most popular sport, but that

    (D) implies that the motorsport is soon supplanting NFL football as the nation's most popular sport, but that

    (E) implies that the motorsport will soon supplant NFL football as the nation's most popular sport, but

LEARNING BY DOING
Slash and Burn Revisited

If you've been following sound sentence correction strategy, you probably noticed the 3-2 split between "implies" and "imply" and slashed and burned your way to the phrase:

The increase ~~in the number~~ ~~of American households~~ ~~viewing telecasts~~ ~~of NASCAR races~~ implies...

"In the number" modifies "increases"; "of American households" modifies "number"; "viewing telecasts" modifies "households"; and "of NASCAR races" modifies "telecasts." "The increase" is the subject of the verb, which must be "implies." That would lead you to eliminate answer choices A and B.

From there, however, there exists quite a bit of reading to do after "implies." Did you also notice the 3-2 split on the back end? You're being asked to decide between "but" and "but that"—a classic sentence construction Decision Point. When you need to decide between connectors, it's helpful to use an offshoot of the slash-and-burn strategy, filling in the details of each portion to be connected with variables to test just that connection:

The increase implies X, but the number of races indicates Y.

vs.

The increase implies X, but that the number of races indicates Y.

The simple "but" is correct and "but that" is wrong. As you can see above, it simply does not provide a parallel connection, so answer choice E is correct.

THINK LIKE THE TESTMAKER
Misdirection

In long sentences such as this, testmakers will purposefully create clever structures so that you miss what really needs to be parallel. Because the verb "implies" is followed by a clause starting with "that," many test-takers will think that the word "that" *is* required to make the structures parallel. However, if you use slash and burn to read the core elements as explained above, it is clear that "that" is incorrect. This is a classic example of misdirection, which is particularly prevalent in long sentences, as it is easier to get lost. **Remember: Be careful about what structures really need to be parallel in any long sentence, and use slash and burn so that you can accurately assess the core structures.**

SKILLS MEET STRATEGY

Focus on Connectors in Long Sentences

The most important takeaway from this problem is: When you see that you have a Decision Point involving connectors, be certain to pounce on it! The authors of the GMAT love connectors; they're small words (but, and, or, because, etc.) that are needles in a haystack in long sentences. But if you know to check them first—particularly when they form the first or last word of the answer choices—then you can make much quicker work of sentences that often take students way too long to assess.

SKILLBUILDER

- Subject-verb agreement
- Sentence construction

17. The success of the new office development will depend not only on the architect's skill in executing his vision of an innovative design, but also the legal team's ability to exercise their claim of eminent domain to secure the waterfront property.

   (A) also the legal team's ability to exercise their claim of eminent domain to secure the waterfront property

   (B) also the legal team's ability to exercise its claim of eminent domain in securing the waterfront property

   (C) also on the legal team's ability to exercise its claim of eminent domain to secure the waterfront property

   (D) also on the legal team's ability to exercise their claim of eminent domain in securing the waterfront property

   (E) on also the legal team's ability to exercise its claim of eminent domain to secure the waterfront property

LEARNING BY DOING

Common Constructions

With popular constructions such as "not only X but (also) Y"; "not X but Y"; "just as X, so (too) Y"; etc., your responsibility is to maintain parallel structure for the two items X and Y. Y (what follows the second set-up of the construction) must be exactly parallel in structure to X. In the example above X (what follows not only) is "on the architect's skill in executing his vision of an innovative design" so what follows must contain the same structure ("on______________"). Given that, it is relatively easy (if you know this rule!) to eliminate answer choices A, B, and E, as they lack this parallel structure (they are missing "on" after "but also"). The choice between answer choices C and D relates to the pronoun "its" vs. "their." Since "legal team" is singular, the pronoun must be "its," and the correct answer choice is thus C.

SKILLS MEET STRATEGY

Strict Parallelism in Common Structures

For common structures, it is essential that you understand this concept of strict parallelism. When you understand this concept, these questions are relatively easy to assess. Consider a few examples to reinforce your understanding:

> *The goal was scored not by Ronaldo, but by Kaka.*

This sentence is correct, because the goal was scored "not by X, but by Y."

Consider another example that lacks parallelism:

> *The goal was scored not by Ronaldo but Kaka.*

This is wrong, because if you stop after "not" and start after "but" you don't have the connector "by":

When you see these constructions, often the key word is the one that precedes "not" or "just." If that word is a preposition/connector (like "by"), then the second half of the construction should not have one, because the "shared" portion of the sentence allocates the connector to both portions:

Taxes are levied by

1. *Not only the state and federal governments*
2. *But also the city and county assessors*

Because the "shared" clause contains "by," it applies to both sections of the construction. But if the connector comes after "not," then each section needs its own "by":

Taxes are levied

1. *Not only by the state and federal governments*
2. *But also by the city and county assessors*

With the common two-part constructions, think about Robert Frost's famous poem. Immediately at the first word of the construction ("not") is where "two roads diverge (in the woods)." And each path must be a complete path that someone could take without having to cross over to the other. That, my friend, will make all the difference....

SKILLBUILDER

- Sentence construction
- Pronouns

LESSON

Sentence Construction: Quick Summary

Most Sentence Correction problems involve longer sentences with substantial underlined portions. To identify sentence construction errors effectively you should focus on the following:

- Slash and burn is a core strategy on long sentence construction problems in which most of the sentence is underlined. **Get rid of unnecessary elements and only read the core structures to see if they are parallel and/or properly linked together.**

- **Parallelism is the most important issue in sentence construction errors.** This is particularly true for the common constructions such as not only/but also, etc.

- **Pay attention to connectors.** Choices in connecting words are often very important in sentence construction errors and can allow you to quickly eliminate two to three otherwise-time-consuming answer choices.

- **Be familiar with the common constructions.** Know the idiomatic expressions (for instance, after range from...to) and understand the strict parallelism required in these constructions.

- **Understand punctuation well.** Make sure you review the Skillbuilder for all sentence construction issues, but punctuation in particular. This can be found on pages 75–83 of the Skillbuilder.

SECTION 3: SENTENCE CORRECTION SUMMARY: PUTTING IT ALL TOGETHER

Sentence correction tests your ability to make decisions, and to do so using a set of core competencies related to grammar and meaning. **To succeed on Sentence Correction problems, avoid the temptation to try to become an expert on all things grammar, and instead focus on these core strategies that you can and will learn to use expertly.** Look for Decision Points, scanning for obvious errors first and emphasizing those that fit within the IMPACTS framework. Remember that your process is to:

1. Briefly scan for obvious IMPACTS differences between answer choices, eliminating choices with "low-hanging fruit" (easy-to-assess Decision Points such as pronoun errors and agreement errors).
2. Read the sentence carefully, mining it for IMPACTS errors. When you find a clear error, go through the answer choices to eliminate each occurrence of that error.
3. Eliminate incorrect answer choices, but *only* when you are absolutely certain that you have found an error.

You should also:

1. Use the slash-and-burn technique to minimize the amount that you have to read.
2. When in doubt, look for subtle differences in meaning between the remaining answer choices.

This last point is critical on difficult questions. The authors of the GMAT love to embed "false" Decision Points in questions to direct you away from subtle changes in meaning. While you dig deep in your memory to try to recall obscure grammar rules or examples of usage, you tend to miss differences that come down much more to logic and problem solving. **Know this about the GMAT: It does not typically make questions harder by testing more-obscure information; instead, it does so by obscuring the existence of decisions that you should be able to expertly make.**

Summary Problem

The IMPACTS checklist is designed to help you better classify and study the common GMAT Decision Points. Strategically, your job is to use slash and burn to streamline sentences so that the Decision Points become more obvious. Often, the first decision that eliminates two or three answer choices will come to you rather naturally, but the second decision between the remaining choices will require you to reflect on the differences between them with an eye for logical meaning. To put all of these strategies together, complete the following problem, which, more than any other you have seen, rewards good strategy:

18. John F. Kennedy, one of the most social U.S. presidents, held many parties in his family home, they featured elaborate meals of local fish and lobster, famous guests, and late nights.

(A) John F. Kennedy, one of the most social U.S. presidents, held many parties in his family home, they featured

(B) Parties were held in one of the most social U.S. president's home, John F. Kennedy, and they featured

(C) John F. Kennedy, who was one of the most social U.S. presidents in his family home, held parties that featured

(D) John F. Kennedy, one of the most social U.S. presidents, held many parties in his family home that featured

(E) In his family home, John F. Kennedy, one of the most social U.S. presidents, held many parties that featured

LEARNING BY DOING

Decision Points and Slash and Burn

As is often the case, there are three answer choices that are relatively easy to eliminate. Answer choice A contains a blatant comma splice, answer choice B contains a blatant modifier error ("home" is modified by John F. Kennedy), and answer choice C creates meaning problems with the location of the prepositional phrases (it suggests he was only a social U.S. president when in his family home). The choice between answer choices D and E is tricky and typical of what you will see on many hard problems. Your gut reaction on a first read-through is probably to pick answer choice D; it seems to read better and is less choppy. **However, on almost all hard Sentence Correction problems, your gut reaction will be proved wrong by good strategy and careful analysis.** One of the key components to slash and burn is the idea of "use it or lose it," which says that you should first assess any modifier for correctness. If the modifier is incorrect, you can eliminate that answer choice; if it's correct, you can remove the modifier from the sentence. The appositive phrase—"one of the most social U.S. presidents"—is used correctly in both answer choices D and E, so you should remove it to reveal your simplified two choices:

(D) John F. Kennedy held many parties in his family home that featured

(E) In his family home, John F. Kennedy held many parties that featured

These answer choices should both sound pretty good to your ear (whereas answer choice E might not have before), so employ good Decision Points strategy: What is the only difference between the two? The location of "in his family home." Now you must figure out why that choice might matter, and in doing so, you should see that there is a problem in answer choice D. Because "that featured..." follows "home," the sentence suggests that the home "featured elaborate meals of local fish and lobster, famous guests, and late nights," and that is clearly illogical. Answer choice E is correct, as it properly positions parties in front of "that featured" and gives clear, logical meaning.

SKILLS MEET STRATEGY

You Don't Have to Do it in a Vacuum

You should remember this problem going forward, as it is a textbook example of how testmakers create difficult Sentence Correction problems. It is also helpful, because it should remind you that sentence correction is primarily about leveraging hints. If you were given answer choice D in a vacuum and asked if it were correct, you would almost surely say yes and miss the modifier problem. But with answer choice E beside it, all you have to do is take the hint and remember some basic tenets of modifier errors. **Remember: On Sentence Correction problems, the hints are always there, but they can be subtle and difficult to leverage. Also, to use those hints, you must have a solid understanding of the core grammar highlighted in the Skillbuilder, so make sure you have that foundation.**

SKILLBUILDER

- Modifiers
- Sentence construction

SECTION 4: YOU OUGHTA KNOW

In this brief "You Oughta Know" section there will be:

1. Several more examples of common construction problems.
2. A discussion of intended meaning vs. logical meaning.
3. More drills for improving slash and burn.

More on Common Constructions

In addition to the "not only...(but) also" structure covered in the "Sentence Construction" section, several other common constructions appear frequently enough on the GMAT that you should expect to see them and should immediately recognize them. These include:

- Just as...so
- Either...or
- Neither...nor
- Range from...to

With these constructions, your job is to ensure that the items ascribed to each are parallel.

19. Just as the Abnaki Indians of Maine joined forces with the French in the 1600s to fight off English settlers and preserve their native hunting and fishing grounds, so the Shawnee Indians of the Midwest joined forces with the British during the War of 1812 to fight off American troops in a last attempt to save its already-embattled traditional territory.

(A) so the Shawnee Indians of the Midwest joined forces with the British during the War of 1812 to fight off American troops in a last attempt to save its already-embattled traditional territory

(B) the Shawnee Indians of the Midwest joined forces with the British during the War of 1812 to fight off American troops in a last attempt to save its already-embattled traditional territory

(C) in a similar fashion, the Shawnee Indians of the Midwest joined forces with the British during the War of 1812 to fight off American troops in a last attempt to save their already-embattled traditional territory

(D) so joined the Shawnee Indians of the Midwest in force with the British during the War of 1812 to fight off American troops in a last attempt to save their already-embattled traditional territory

(E) so the Shawnee Indians of the Midwest joined forces with the British during the War of 1812 to fight off American troops in a last attempt to save their already-embattled traditional territory

20. Ansel Adams's passion for the environment is evident in photographs that range from majestic landscapes of snow-capped mountain ranges across the American west, particularly in his home state of California, <u>and</u> simple images of lone trees and blossoming flowers wherever the beauty of nature struck him.

    (A) and

    (B) to

    (C) and to

    (D) in addition to

    (E) with

LEARNING BY DOING

Know the Expressions and Focus on Parallelism

In both of these problems, you must be familiar with the structural idiomatic expressions being used. The first one is "just as…so" and the second is "range from…to." In the first example (#19), you can eliminate answer choices B and C because they lack the necessary "so" to complete the expression. Then you should look for other Decision Points. The most obvious one is the fact that in answer choice D "so" is followed by the verb "joined," while in answer choices A and E it is followed by the noun "the Shawnee Indians." Leveraging what you learned earlier about these common constructions, you know that what follows "just as" in structure must follow "so" in structure. Answer choice D violates this parallelism by putting a verb where the noun should be, so you can eliminate it. The final Decision Point between answer choices A and E is a pronoun that is easy to miss: "its" in answer choice A vs. "their" in answer choice E. Since the pronoun is referring back to the Shawnee Indians (plural) then it must be "their," and answer choice E is correct.

The second problem (#20) is much simpler, as long as you know the proper expression and you slash and burn the many modifiers in the sentence. After getting rid of unnecessary modifiers and other unnecessary words, you see that this sentence is really "photographs that range from X ????? Y." Given that structure, it must be "range from X to Y," so the correct answer choice is B.

SKILLBUILDER

- Sentence construction—parallelism
- Sentence construction—common constructions
- Pronouns

Intended Meaning vs. Illogical Meaning

If you have not yet encountered the term "intended meaning" in your GMAT study, you are free—and encouraged—to skip this page! But if you have, this point is worth learning. While many GMAT books and websites—including the Official Guide for GMAT Review in some of its solutions—provide as rationale for eliminating answer choices that they "distort the intended meaning" of the sentence, beware that the concept of "intended meaning" is dangerous if you use it to solve problems. Consider, as evidence, the following answer choices from an official GMAT problem:

(A) Using a Doppler ultrasound device, fetal heartbeats can be detected by the twelfth week of pregnancy.

(E) Using a Doppler ultrasound device, a physician can detect fetal heartbeats by the twelfth week of pregnancy. (CORRECT)

Using the concept of "intended meaning," one might argue that, while grammatically preferable, answer choice E distorts the meaning by adding "a physician" to the sentence. But that argument misses the point of this exercise; answer choice A is incorrect because the modifier "Using a Doppler ultrasound device" needs to describe an actor who can use such a device. The sentence as written does not supply a logical actor, whereas the corrected answer choice E does. Answer choice E changes—or at least adds to—the meaning of answer choice A, but that is perfectly acceptable. **Do not ascribe any "incumbency" to answer choice A**; if answer choice A is illogical, then the correct answer must change the meaning.

The problem with the concept of intended meaning is that it seems to suggest that a sentence can mean something other than what it explicitly says. In fact, the dominant strategy for Sentence Correction is to recognize that each sentence means exactly what it says, and so if that meaning is illogical, the sentence *must* be changed. Your job on the GMAT is not to play mind reader and try to interpret what a sentence might mean; your job is to judge each sentence on what it says, and to eliminate illogical meanings.

More Drills for Slash and Burn

As you learned in the lesson, slash and burn is an essential tool in GMAT Sentence Correction. Before you attack the homework problems, practice slash and burn with five more drills, eliminating all clutter and changing any verbs that do not agree with their subjects.

1. Such an organization may, for instance, aim to educate the public as to what the difference between two candidates' positions on a set of issues are, but are prohibited from exhibiting bias designed to influence prospective voters to favor a particular candidate.

2. A fund has been established to aid in the rebuilding efforts that will begin this weekend, and residents who are able to contribute in money or labor to the project are encouraged to do so.

3. Indeed, these terms have given rise to international tourist attractions: in front of the Frankfurt Stock Exchange stand imposing bronze bull and bear statues, and New York's Bowling Green and Shanghai's Bund Financial Square feature "Charging Bull" sculptures that attract throngs at all times of the year.

4. As of now, the coalition of local environmental groups have resolved to continue to protest the expansion of the campus into what is presently woodland abutting it.

5. Still under discussion are the issue of whether, in light of recent setbacks, its efforts should remain essentially non-disruptive in nature and the possibility of calling upon national environmental champions to endorse the campaign.

Slash and Burn Drill Solutions

1. Such an organization may, ~~for instance~~, aim to educate the public as to what the difference ~~between two candidates' positions on a set of issues~~ IS, but IS prohibited ~~from exhibiting bias designed to influence prospective voters to favor a particular candidate~~.

2. A fund has been established to aid ~~in the rebuilding efforts that will begin this weekend~~, and residents ~~who are able to contribute in money or labor to the project~~ are encouraged to do so.

3. ~~Indeed~~, these terms have given rise ~~to international tourist attractions~~: ~~in front of the Frankfurt Stock Exchange~~ stand ~~imposing bronze bull and bear~~ statues, and ~~New York's~~ Bowling Green and ~~Shanghai's~~ Bund Financial Square feature ~~"Charging Bull"~~ sculptures ~~that attract throngs at all times of the year~~.

4. ~~As of now~~, the coalition ~~of local environmental groups~~ HAS resolved to continue to protest the expansion ~~of the campus into what is presently woodland abutting it~~.

5. ~~Still under discussion~~ are the issue ~~of whether, in light of recent setbacks, its efforts should remain essentially non-disruptive in nature~~ and the possibility ~~of calling upon national environmental champions to endorse the campaign~~.

HOMEWORK

21. Known globally as one of the greatest musical acts of all time, The Beatles recorded 20 singles that reached the top spot on the *Billboard* charts; their songs, including "Yesterday", which spent four weeks in the top spot, have been covered more often than any modern band.

    (A) than any

    (B) than any other

    (C) compared to those of any

    (D) than those of any other

    (E) as have those of any

22. Setting a precedent that lasted more than a century, George Washington disappointed the people insisting that he should run for a third term as president.

    (A) insisting that he should

    (B) insisting him to

    (C) and their insistence that he

    (D) who insisted that he

    (E) who insisted him to

23. Unlike cellular phones and personal computers, there is a difficulty on the part of many people to adapt to other modern technologies.

(A) Unlike cellular phones and personal computers, there is a difficulty on the part of many people to adapt to other modern technologies.

(B) Unlike cellular phones and personal computers, which many people are comfortable using, they have difficulty adapting to other modern technologies.

(C) Unlike cellular phones and personal computers, other modern technologies bring out a difficulty for many people to adapt to them.

(D) Many people, though comfortable using cellular phones and personal computers, have difficulty adapting to other modern technologies.

(E) Many people have a difficulty in adapting to other modern technologies, while they are comfortable using cellular phones and personal computers.

24. A recent research study of worldwide cellular penetration finds that there are now one mobile phone for every two people, more than twice as many than there were in 2005.

(A) there are now one mobile phone for every two people, more than twice as many than there were

(B) there is now one mobile phone for every two people, more than twice as many than there were

(C) there is now one mobile phone for every two people, more than twice as many as there were

(D) every two people now have one mobile phone, more than twice as many than there were

(E) every two people now has one mobile phone, more than twice as many as there were

25. In 1972 votes were cast by fifty-five percent of the electorate; and forty percent in 1996.

(A) electorate; and forty percent in 1996

(B) electorate; in 1996 the figure was forty percent

(C) electorate, and in 1996 forty percent

(D) electorate, forty percent in 1996 was the figure

(E) electorate that fell to forty percent in 1996

26. <u>Like Bob Dylan, the music of Talib Kweli</u> is a social commentary—lyrics and instrumentals designed to tell stories and inspire thought about the world in which the artist lives.

(A) Like Bob Dylan, the music of Talib Kweli

(B) Like Bob Dylan, Talib Kweli's music

(C) Like Bob Dylan's, Talib Kweli's music

(D) As with Bob Dylan, Talib Kwelil's music

(E) As is Bob Dylan's, the music of Talib Kweli

27. Growing out of a need for affordable housing during the Great Depression, the first student housing cooperatives were structured as not-for-profit organizations, whose members made small payments toward their room and board, then taking turns performing household duties, such as meal preparation and property maintenance.

(A) board, then taking turns performing

(B) board, and then taking turns performing

(C) board and then took turns performing

(D) board and then took turns, they performed

(E) board and then took turns and performed

28. Although Belize borders Guatemala and Mexico, countries in which tortillas are served with nearly every dish, Belizeans typically eat their meals with rice, and tortillas are rare.

(A) Belizeans typically eat their meals with rice, and tortillas are rare

(B) Belizeans typically eat its meals with rice, and tortillas are rare

(C) Belizeans typically eat its meals with rice, with tortillas as rare

(D) Belizeans typically eat their meals with rice, tortillas a rarity

(E) Belizeans typically eat their meals with rice, with tortillas as a rarity

29. Surprised by unexpected budgetary constraints, it was chosen by the department managers to cancel the office New Year's party.

(A) it was chosen by the department managers to cancel the office New Year's party

(B) the choice of the department managers was to cancel the office New Year's party

(C) the department managers chose to cancel the office New Year's party

(D) the office New Year's party was canceled by the department managers

(E) a cancellation was chosen for the New Year's party by the department managers

30. The decrease in the willingness of banks to make loans to home buyers and small business owners have created a downward economic spiral, as home prices are plummeting, businesses are reluctant to create jobs, and consumers are avoiding nonessential purchases.

(A) have created

(B) are creating

(C) had created

(D) has created

(E) creates

31. In an unprecedented display of bipartisanship, the House of Representatives are expected to unanimously approve a bill that will result in as many appropriations for national parks as have been made during the last four administrations combined.

   (A) are expected to unanimously approve a bill that will result in as many appropriations for national parks as have been made during the last four administrations combined

   (B) is expected to unanimously approve a bill that will result in as many appropriations for national parks than have been made during the last four administrations combined

   (C) are expected to unanimously approve a bill that will result in as many appropriations for national parks than have been made during the last four administrations combined

   (D) is expected to unanimously approve a bill that will result in as many appropriations for national parks as have been made during the last four administrations combined

   (E) is expected to unanimously approve a bill that will result in as many appropriations for national parks as the last four administrations combined

32. As its winning percentage has dwindled, the team has become increasingly willing to sign players <u>they would in the past have ignored</u>.

(A) they would in the past have ignored

(B) they would have ignored previously

(C) that in the past would have been ignored previously

(D) it previously would have ignored in the past

(E) it would in the past have ignored

33. Auditors perform a key function in business: <u>not only are the validity and reliability of financial statements needed to be ascertained by them, but also on performing</u> assessments of a company's internal control.

(A) not only are the validity and reliability of financial statements needed to be ascertained by them, but also on performing

(B) they not only ascertain the validity and reliability of financial statements for public use, but also perform

(C) the validity and reliability of financial statements not only needs to be ascertained by them, but also they perform

(D) not only the validity and reliability of financial statements need to be ascertained by them, but also on performing

(E) the validity and reliability needs to be ascertained not only on financial statements, but also they perform

34. Of all the events leading to the formation of the Earth, the catalyst for the infinite mass of matter that caused the Big Bang is maybe the more difficult for determination.

(A) is maybe the more difficult for determination

(B) is probably the most difficult to determine

(C) is maybe the most difficult for determination

(D) is probably the more difficult to determine

(E) is, it may be, the determination that is most difficult

35. The question of whether to allocate a portion of their salaries to retirement plans is particularly troublesome for recent college graduates, whose salaries are typically lower <u>than</u> senior members of companies; with the rising cost of living, younger employees often struggle with having to pay bills while trying to save for the long run.

    (A) than

    (B) than those of

    (C) than is so of

    (D) compared to

    (E) compared to those of

36. Because of dramatic improvements in computing technology, $200 today buys <u>double the hard drive space that it has</u> in 2004.

(A) double the hard drive space that it has

(B) double the hard drive space that it did

(C) as much as twice the hard drive space it has

(D) two times as many hard drive space as there were

(E) a doubling of the hard drive space that it did

37. Having one of the highest melting points of all the chemical elements, tungsten is used in temperature-dependent products such as light bulb filaments so adaptable that it is also used to make wedding bands.

(A) filaments so adaptable

(B) filaments being so adaptable

(C) filaments, yet being so adaptable

(D) filaments, and so adaptable

(E) filaments yet is so adaptable

38. Turn-of-the-century magician Harry Houdini claimed, for his famous water-torture cell trick, the ability to hold his breath for more than three minutes.

(A) the ability to hold his breath

(B) he has the ability of holding his breath

(C) the ability of him holding his breath

(D) to be able to hold his breath

(E) being able to hold his breath

39. The demand for professors in highly vocational fields like business, law, and the applied sciences remain strong despite a difficult job market for most PhD graduates seeking to teach in academia.

(A) fields like business, law, and the applied sciences remain

(B) fields like those of business, law, and the applied sciences remain

(C) fields such as business, law, and the applied sciences remains

(D) fields such as business, law, and the applied sciences remain

(E) fields, like the fields of business, law, and the applied sciences, remains

40. Additional incentives to teach in the inner cities, <u>such as tuition reimbursement, is</u> giving prospective teachers more to consider when planning where to settle.

(A) such as tuition reimbursement, is

(B) like tuition reimbursement, is

(C) tuition reimbursement being one, is

(D) like tuition reimbursement, are

(E) such as tuition reimbursement, are

41. Using a new, high-technology process, diamonds can be created by simulating the natural processes that occur over time in the Earth's crust.

    (A) Using a new, high-technology process, diamonds can be created by simulating the natural processes that occur over time in the Earth's crust.

    (B) Diamonds can be created by simulating the natural processes that occur over time in the Earth's crust, using a new, high-technology process.

    (C) Creating diamonds by simulating the natural processes that occur over time in the Earth's crust, scientists can use a new, high-technology process.

    (D) By simulating the natural processes that occur over time in the Earth's crust, diamonds can be created using a new, high-technology process by a scientist.

    (E) Using a new, high-technology process, scientists can create diamonds by simulating the natural processes that occur over time in the Earth's crust.

42. A newly discovered letter by Jonathan Swift, written in the same year as *Gulliver's Travels* were published, shows how the biting satire that marked many of Swift's public works was reflected in his private writings as well.

(A) A newly discovered letter by Jonathan Swift, written in the same year as *Gulliver's Travels* were published

(B) A newly discovered letter by Jonathan Swift, written in the same year of publication as *Gulliver's Travels*

(C) A newly discovered letter by Jonathan Swift, written in the same year that *Gulliver's Travels* was published

(D) Jonathan Swift wrote a newly discovered letter in the same year as he published *Gulliver's Travels* that

(E) Jonathan Swift wrote a newly discovered letter in the same year of publication as *Gulliver's Travels* that

43. Unlike its modern-day status as bioethically impermissible, lobotomy was initially hailed as a revolutionary therapeutic technique so much that the Portuguese neurologist Egas Moniz who introduced the procedure was in fact awarded the Nobel Prize in Medicine in 1949 for his contribution.

(A) Unlike its modern-day status as bioethically impermissible, lobotomy was initially hailed as a revolutionary therapeutic technique so much that the Portuguese neurologist Egas Moniz who introduced the procedure was

(B) Despite its modern-day status as bioethically impermissible, lobotomy was initially hailed as a revolutionary therapeutic technique; and along with the Portuguese neurologist Egas Moniz who introduced the procedure was

(C) Despite its modern-day status as bioethically impermissible, lobotomy was initially hailed as a revolutionary therapeutic technique; Egas Moniz, the Portuguese neurologist who introduced the procedure, was

(D) Unlike its modern-day status as bioethically impermissible, that of lobotomy initially was hailed as a revolutionary technique, such that Egas Moniz, the Portuguese neurologist who introduced the procedure, was

(E) In contrast to its modern-day status as bioethically impermissible, the initial status of lobotomy was hailed as a revolutionary technique; Egas Moniz, the Portuguese neurologist who introduced the procedure, was

44. Perhaps nowhere else in America can one see a greater span of architectural history than on Ivy League campuses with their blend of the classic and the contemporary, each of the campus buildings a monument to the era in which it was built.

(A) each of the campus buildings a monument to the era in which it was

(B) all of the campus buildings a monument to the era in which they were

(C) all of the campus buildings a monument to the era in which it was

(D) every campus building a monument to the era in which they were

(E) each of the campus buildings a monument to the era in which they were

45. Unlike traditional retailers that deploy one new product line per season, delivering new looks every few weeks has enabled fast fashion clothing retailers to respond to fluctuations in demand and media events and stay ahead of the competition.

(A) delivering new looks every few weeks has enabled fast fashion clothing retailers to respond to fluctuations in demand and media events and stay

(B) fast fashion clothing retailers deliver new looks every few weeks, enabling them to respond to fluctuations in demand and media events, and stay

(C) the delivering of new looks every few weeks has enabled fast fashion clothing retailers to respond to fluctuations in demand and media events, staying

(D) fast fashion clothing retailers, by delivering new looks every few weeks, have been able to respond to media events and fluctuations in demand and stay

(E) fast fashion clothing retailers, by delivering new looks every few weeks, have been able to respond to fluctuations in demand and media events and stayed

46. Already anxious after watching a horror movie, Michele mistook the sound of a backfiring car as the blast of a gunshot.

(A) the sound of a backfiring car as the blast of a gunshot

(B) a car as it was backfiring for the blast of a gunshot

(C) the sound of a backfiring car for the blast of a gunshot

(D) a car as it was backfiring as the blast of a gunshot

(E) a backfiring car as the blast of a gunshot

47. Politicians and philosophers, early forms of democratic government and public discourse were pioneered by the ancient Greeks, laying the groundwork for much of modern society.

(A) early forms of democratic government and public discourse were pioneered by the ancient Greeks, laying the groundwork for much of modern society

(B) laying the groundwork for much of modern society, early forms of democratic government and public discourse were pioneered by the ancient Greeks

(C) the ancient Greeks pioneered early forms of democratic government and public discourse, laying the groundwork for much of modern society

(D) there were pioneered, laying the groundwork for much of modern society, early forms of democratic government and public discourse by the ancient Greeks

(E) were the ancient Greeks who, laying the groundwork for much of modern society, pioneered early forms of democratic government and public discourse

48. Like many famous jazz trumpet players, John Birks "Dizzy" Gillespie played many other musical instruments, including the piano.

(A) Like

(B) As have

(C) Just as with

(D) Just like

(E) As did

49. Supply-side economists theorize that large-capital firms find the need to declare bankruptcy more due to the fact that they become burdened with high operating costs than failure to compete for consumer demand.

(A) due to the fact that they become burdened with high operating costs than failure

(B) due to their becoming burdened with high operating costs than to failing

(C) because they become burdened with high operating costs than that they fail

(D) because they become burdened with high operating costs than because they fail

(E) because of their becoming burdened with high operating costs than because of their

50. <u>Selling two hundred thousand copies in its first month, the publication of *The Audacity of Hope* in 2006 was an instant hit, helping to establish Barack Obama as a viable candidate for president.</u>

(A) Selling two hundred thousand copies in its first month, the publication of *The Audacity of Hope* in 2006 was an instant hit, helping to establish Barack Obama as a viable candidate for president.

(B) The publication in 2006 of *The Audacity of Hope* was an instant hit: in its first month it sold two hundred thousand copies and it helped establish Barack Obama as a viable candidate for president.

(C) Helping to establish Barack Obama as a viable candidate for president was the publication of *The Audacity of Hope* in 2006, which as an instant hit: it sold two hundred thousand copies in its first month.

(D) *The Audacity of Hope* was an instant hit: it helped establish Barack Obama as a viable candidate for president, selling two hundred thousand copies in its first month and published in 2006.

(E) *The Audacity of Hope*, published in 2006, was an instant hit: in its first month, it sold two hundred thousand copies and helped establish its author, Barack Obama, as a viable candidate for president.

51. Because of limited available funds, some non-profit companies <u>had elected to train their current employees in management techniques rather than recruiting</u> knowledgeable managers from outside sources.

(A) had elected to train their current employees in management techniques rather than recruiting

(B) had elected training current employees in management techniques rather than recruiting

(C) have elected training current employees in management techniques instead of recruiting

(D) have elected to train current employees in management techniques rather than recruiting

(E) have elected to train current employees in management techniques rather than recruit

52. Visitors to the zoo have often looked up in to the leafy aviary and saw macaws resting on the branches, whose tails trail like brightly colored splatters of paint on a green canvas.

(A) saw macaws resting on the branches, whose tails trail

(B) saw macaws resting on the branches, whose tails were trailing

(C) saw macaws resting on the branches, with tails trailing

(D) seen macaws resting on the branches, with tails trailing

(E) seen macaws resting on the branches, whose tails have trailed

53. The North American bald eagle is no longer threatened with imminent extinction, primarily on account of prohibiting hunting and the ban of a poisonous pesticide have led to a rebound in the eagle population.

(A) on account of prohibiting

(B) on account of their prohibiting

(C) because prohibitions on

(D) because of prohibiting

(E) because they prohibit

54. <u>Although severely damaged in the hurricane, the captain was able to repair</u> the generator so that it could power the hospital until the city's electricity was restored.

(A) Although severely damaged in the hurricane, the captain was able to repair

(B) Although severely damaged in the hurricane, the captain had repaired

(C) Although it had been severely damaged in the hurricane, the captain was able to repair

(D) Severely damaged though it had been in the hurricane, the captain had been able to repair

(E) Damaged severely in the hurricane, the captain was able to repair

55. Since 1945, the United Nations, an organization with 192 member <u>states has worked to promote economic development and it is</u> an important international issue.

(A) states has worked to promote economic development and it is

(B) states, which has worked to promote economic development, is

(C) states, has worked to promote economic development,

(D) states has worked to promote economic development, being

(E) states, has worked to promote economic development, and is

56. Astronomers of the late twentieth century discovered several distant, planet-like objects orbiting the sun, which has led to heated debates over which of these objects are deserving the classification "planet."

(A) which has led to heated debates over which of these objects are deserving

(B) leading to heated debates over which of these objects deserve

(C) which has led to heated debates over which of these objects should deserve

(D) leading to heated debates over which of these objects are deserving

(E) which is now leading to heated debates over which of these objects deserve

57. Sulfur dioxide, which smells like rotten eggs, <u>is formed in smokestacks from</u> sulfur and oxygen, two of the major elements consumed in coal smelting, react with each other.

(A) is formed in smokestacks from

(B) is formed in smokestacks when

(C) is formed in smokestacks, and when

(D) formed in smokestacks when

(E) formed in smokestacks from

58. John Kennedy and his Cabinet met in October 1962 to consider a possible Russian effort to station weaponry in Cuba and how they would have to act militarily to deal with them.

(A) how they would have to act militarily to deal with them

(B) how to deal with them if military action would be necessary

(C) what would be necessary militarily for dealing with such an event

(D) what military action would be necessary in order to deal with such an event

(E) the necessity of what kind of military action to take in order for dealing with it

59. The tornado left a path of destruction in its wake, causing the collapse of several homes, massive power outages, <u>tearing apart construction projects</u>, and widespread business closures.

(A) tearing apart construction projects

(B) the tearing apart of construction projects

(C) tore apart construction projects

(D) construction projects torn apart

(E) construction projects that were torn apart

60. The United States had never previously experienced so many electoral disputes at once as it had in the storied 1876 presidential election, in which Rutherford B. Hayes was ultimately named the winner.

(A) so many electoral disputes at once as it had in

(B) at once as many electoral disputes as

(C) at once as many electoral disputes that there were with

(D) as many electoral disputes at once as it experienced in

(E) as many electoral disputes at once as it had experienced in

61. Much of the basin that had been transformed into the Great Lakes by the Laurentide Glacier during the last ice age was formed by seismological events that occurred nearly one billion years earlier.

(A) Much of the basin that had been transformed into the Great Lakes by the Laurentide Glacier during the last ice age was

(B) Much of the basin that was transformed into the Great Lakes by the Laurentide Glacier during the last ice age had been

(C) Much of the basin that was transformed into the Great Lakes by the Laurentide Glacier during the last ice age has been

(D) The Laurentide Glacier during the last ice age transformed the Great Lakes from much of the basin that has been

(E) During the last ice age, much of the basin that was transformed by the Laurentide Glacier into the Great Lakes had been

62. Ironically, <u>before he shot and killed</u> Abraham Lincoln at Ford's Theatre, John Wilkes Booth had performed in front of the president in the very same venue.

(A) before he shot and killed

(B) before the shooting and killing of

(C) before he had shot and killed

(D) prior to when he shot and killed

(E) prior to the shooting and killing of

63. Many companies require that every employee be reviewed by his or her superior twice per year.

(A) require that every employee be reviewed by his or her superior

(B) require that every employee to be reviewed by his or her superior

(C) require that every employee will be reviewed by his or her superior

(D) have a requirement for an employee review

(E) have a requirement to review every employee

64. When the SARS (Severe Acute Respiratory Syndrome) pandemic occurred in late 2002, officials feared that the outbreak would be widespread; they were concerned that the virus would become a global threat and it would kill vast numbers of patients who would have no protection against it.

(A) it would kill vast numbers of patients who would have no protection against it

(B) it would kill vast numbers of patients with no protection against it

(C) kill vast numbers of patients who would have no protection against it

(D) kill vast numbers of patients who have no protection against them

(E) kill vast numbers of patients with no protection against them

65. Independent theaters in Philadelphia have largely abandoned the production of Broadway touring shows and now they often showcase the talents both of local artists who write about local issues and those about broader topics.

(A) now they often showcase the talents both of local artists who write about local issues and those

(B) now often showcase the talents of local artists, both those who write about local issues and those who write

(C) they often showcase the talents of local artists now, both those writing about local issues and who write

(D) often showcase now the talents both of local artists writing about local issues and who are writing

(E) often showcase the talents of both local artists writing about local issues and those

66. One immediate legacy of America's recent mortgage crisis is the realization that credit may never again be so easily available.

(A) is the realization that credit may never again be so easily available

(B) are the realizations that credit may never again be so easily available

(C) is realizing that credit may never again be so easily available

(D) is to realize that credit may never again be so easily available

(E) is realizing that credit will never again be so easily available

67. The beautiful cello solo at the end of the symphony may have salvaged the performance, <u>for most of the orchestra members performed poorly throughout the two hour concert</u>.

(A) for most of the orchestra members performed poorly throughout the two hour concert

(B) in that most of the orchestra members performed throughout the two hour concert in a poor manner

(C) when most of the orchestra members performed poorly throughout the two hour concert

(D) despite most of the orchestra members performing poorly throughout the two hour concert

(E) even though most of the orchestra members made a poor performance throughout the two hour concert

68. In the 2008 Wimbledon final, Rafael Nadal beat Roger Federer in 5 sets, shocking the tennis world and winning his first Grand Slam tournament other than the French Open title, which he already won 4 times.

(A) In the 2008 Wimbledon final, Rafael Nadal beat Roger Federer in 5 sets, shocking the tennis world and winning his first Grand Slam tournament other than the French Open title, which he already won 4 times.

(B) In the 2008 Wimbledon final, Rafael Nadal beat Roger Federer in 5 sets, shocked the tennis world, and won his first Grand Slam tournament other than the French Open title, which he had already won 4 times.

(C) In the 2008 Wimbledon final, Rafael Nadal beat Roger Federer in 5 sets, shocked the tennis world, and he won his first Grand Slam tournament other than the French Open title, which he had already won 4 times.

(D) In the 2008 Wimbledon final, Rafael Nadal beat Roger Federer in 5 sets, shocking the tennis world and winning his first Grand Slam tournament other than the French Open, which he had already won 4 times.

(E) In the 2008 Wimbledon final, Rafael Nadal beat Roger Federer in 5 sets, which shocked the tennis world and gave him his first Grand Slam tournament other than the French Open, which he had already won 4 times.

69. Sir Arthur Conan Doyle's book *The Coming of the Fairies* revealed <u>that this creator of the famous detective Sherlock Holmes, who valued reason above all other qualities, was a spiritualist affected in both his private life and</u> his friendships by his belief in psychic phenomena.

(A) that this creator of the famous detective Sherlock Holmes, who valued reason above all other qualities, was a spiritualist affected in both his private life and

(B) that this creator of the famous detective Sherlock Holmes, who valued reason above all other qualities, was a spiritualist and also affected in both his private life and

(C) this creator of the famous detective Sherlock Holmes, who valued reason above all other qualities, was a spiritualist and that he was affected in both his private life and

(D) this creator of the famous detective Sherlock Holmes, who valued reason above all other qualities, was a spiritualist and that he was affected in both his private life as well as

(E) this creator of the most famous detective Sherlock Holmes, who valued reason above all other qualities, to have been a spiritualist and that he affected himself both in his private life as well as

70. From the first-class wait staff to the exotic dishes and the ornate silverware, everything about the banquet was designed to impress, and it is.

(A) was designed to impress, and it is

(B) is designed to impress, and it has

(C) is designed to impress, and it does

(D) is being designed to impress, and it has

(E) had been designed to impress, and it has

71. A booming population center, the Asian continent is home to over 3.5 billion people, about <u>equivalent to the residents of</u> all the other areas of the world combined.

(A) equivalent to the residents of

(B) the equivalent of those residing in

(C) equal to those who reside in

(D) as many as the residents of

(E) as many as reside in

72. The Buffalo Club has approved tenets mandating <u>that members should volunteer time</u> to aid the community.

(A) that members should volunteer time

(B) that time be volunteered by members

(C) the volunteering of time by members

(D) members' volunteering of time

(E) that members volunteer time

73. Unlike the terms served by Grover Cleveland, separated by four years, all former two-term U.S. Presidents have served consecutive terms.

    (A) Unlike the terms served by Grover Cleveland, separated by four years

    (B) Besides the terms of Grover Cleveland that were separated by four years

    (C) Except for Grover Cleveland, whose terms were separated by four years

    (D) Aside from the terms of Grover Cleveland that were separated by four years

    (E) Other than the separated terms of Grover Cleveland, of four years

74. Many professional football teams have found that they are better served by selecting linemen in the college draft instead of selecting skill position players, such as wide receivers and quarterbacks, who tend to demand higher salaries and who take longer to develop into quality players at the professional level.

(A) they are better served by selecting linemen in the college draft instead of selecting

(B) selecting linemen in the college draft better serves them than the selection of

(C) they are better served by selecting linemen in the college draft rather than by selecting

(D) the selection of linemen is better than

(E) they are better served by selecting linemen in the college draft than by selecting

75. Featured in circuses for more than a century, trapeze artists hang from swings by the ankles and perform acrobatic maneuvers, rebalancing frequently enough that spectators see only his continuous, fluid movement.

    (A) trapeze artists hang from swings by the ankles and perform acrobatic maneuvers, rebalancing frequently enough

    (B) trapeze artists hang from swings by the ankles, they perform acrobatic maneuvers, and with such frequent rebalancing

    (C) trapeze artists use their ankles to hang from swings, perform acrobatic maneuvers, and rebalance so frequently that

    (D) the trapeze artist hangs from swings by his ankles, performing acrobatic maneuvers and rebalancing so frequently

    (E) the trapeze artist hangs from swings by his ankles, performs acrobatic maneuvers, and he rebalances frequently enough

ANSWER KEY

LESSONS		HOMEWORK			
1. D	17. C	21. D	37. E	53. C	69. A
2. E	18. E	22. D	38. D	54. C	70. C
3. D	19. E	23. D	39. C	55. C	71. E
4. C	20. B	24. C	40. E	56. B	72. E
5. D		25. B	41. E	57. B	73. C
6. C		26. C	42. C	58. D	74. E
7. D		27. C	43. C	59. B	75. D
8. C		28. E	44. A	60. D	
9. D		29. C	45. D	61. B	
10. B		30. D	46. C	62. A	
11. A		31. D	47. C	63. A	
12. D		32. E	48. A	64. C	
13. B		33. B	49. D	65. B	
14. A		34. B	50. E	66. A	
15. E		35. B	51. E	67. A	
16. E		36. B	52. D	68. D